Sauerkraut, Kimchi, Pickles & Relishes

Your Passport to a Healthy and Happy Life

Stanley Marianski, Adam Marianski

Bookmagic, LLC
Seminole, Florida

Contents

ISBN: 978-0-9836973-2-9
Library of Congress Control Number: 2012902778

Bookmagic, LLC.
http://www.bookmagic.com

Printed in the United States of America.

Introduction

There has never been a greater consumer awareness about the food we eat. High blood pressure and cholesterol levels are increasing, half of us will develop some kind of cancer and obesity is a huge concern. What is of special concern is the number of young adults who are obese and getting sick. Most of them will be unhappy for the rest of their lives and will become a burden on the health system. Fast food establishments kill our children with fries, sodas, burgers, desserts and the portions are getting bigger.

Our lifestyle has changed, we sit in front of computers or televisions hours every day, nibbling on potato chips and high caloric snacks. We cook less at home as in most cases we warm up commercially prepared foods that we buy in a local supermarket. The modern Western society is getting weaker and sicker by the minute.

Consumers are more educated now and are increasingly aware of the link between fat intake, excess weight and heart disease. The benefits of a diet rich in vegetables are well known. Unfortunately, most commercially produced foods are heated and that step eliminates many of the beneficial bacteria, vitamins and nutrients which are so needed by our body. We end up eating a product with a familiar flavor, but with a little nutritional value. However, the majority of the healthiest vegetables, for example cabbage, beets and radishes, can be fermented without involving thermal processing. This will not only preserve the original value of the nutrients, but will increase the count of beneficial bacteria, changing the character of the vegetable to a probiotic.

Probiotics are live microorganisms that are beneficial to the host organism. The best example is sauerkraut which was crucial to the survival of people in harsh winters in Northern Europe. Once its benefits were better understood, it was required to be on board of every sea going vessel, whether commercial or the Royal Navy. This daily serving of sauerkraut had eliminated scurvy disease and saved the lives of countless seamen.

Korean kimchi has been credited with preventing severe acute respiratory syndrome (SARS), a serious form of pneumonia. It is caused by a virus that was first identified in 2003. Korea has managed to stay SARS-free and some are saying that the reason for this can be found in kimchi.

One does not need to become a vegetarian in order to receive benefits from eating vegetables, but one should eat them often. Vegetables contain very few calories yet are loaded with all the minerals and vitamins that our body needs to function well. A point to remember is that home manufactured products which are not thermally heated offer more benefits than a commercially pasteurized product.

Adam Marianski

All About Cabbage

Photo 1.1 White cabbage.

Photo 1.2 White cabbage head.

Photo 1.3 White cabbage cross section.

Cabbage has been fermented in many areas of the world. Cabbage in all of its forms has always been popular in Europe and we find cabbage soup, stuffed cabbage with meat and rice, or sauerkraut with meat and potatoes. It tastes great when served with a grilled sausage and you can find street carts that serve hotdogs with sauerkraut in the USA as well. Early German immigrants introduced cabbage and traditional sauerkraut recipes into the United States. As a result German soldiers and people of German descent were often referred to as "krauts." Cabbage belongs to the food family traditionally known as cruciferous vegetables and is related to kale, broccoli, collards and Brussel sprouts.

There are five major cabbage varieties:

1. Western cabbage white, scientific name: *Brassica oleracea (Capitata Group)*, this variety is used for making German or Eastern European sauerkraut. Western white cabbage is also called green cabbage or Dutch White. The color of green cabbage ranges from pale to dark green. Both green and red cabbage have *smooth-textured* leaves. It is difficult to pinpoint the exact origin of the headed cabbage that we know today, but we know that the cultivation of cabbage spread across northern Europe into Germany, Poland and Russia, where it became a very popular vegetable.

2. Western cabbage red, scientific name: *Brassica oleracea (Capitata Group)*, has leaves that are either crimson or purple with white veins running through it. Red cabbage tastes just like green cabbage, so your choice between them depends largely on which color you prefer. The product of red cabbage fermentation is known as red kraut or blue kraut after preparation. Keep in mind that red cabbage tends to bleed and *discolor* surrounding foods. Red cabbage is sweeter and contains more nutrients than other cabbage types. Red and green cabbage have a stronger flavor and crunchy texture as compared to Savoy and napa cabbages.

Photo 1.4 Red cabbage.

Photo 1.5 Red cabbage cross section.

3. Savoy cabbage, scientific name: *Brassica oleracea (Capitata Group),* a flavorful crinkled leaf cabbage, is one of the best varieties for cooking. Its head consists of loose leaves, which vary in color from dark green to light green containing lacy patterned veins. It goes well with red wine, apples, spices, horseradish and meat. Savoy cabbage is like ordinary cabbage, but with a milder flavor. The leaves of Savoy cabbage are more ruffled and yellowish-green in color.

Photo 1.6 Savoy cabbage.

Photo 1.7 Savoy cabbage.

Photo 1.8 Savoy cabbage cross section.

A variety of the savoy cabbage is the January King Cabbage. The January King was a favorite variety in Victorian times and is still considered in England to be the finest cabbage of them all. January King is not quite a savoy, and not quite as smooth as Western cabbage; not quite red and not quite green; it combines the most attractive features of all those cabbages. This is a hardy winter cabbage, not even severe frost seems to bother it. The heads are crisp and crunchy and with good flavor, the leaf is a conifer-blue color.

4. Chinese cabbage, has a milder flavor, more delicate texture and contains more water. This cabbage comes in two distinct varieties, both related to the Western cabbage:

A. Chinese cabbage, (pe-tsai), scientific name: *Brassica rapa (Pekinensis Group)*, also known as **Napa** cabbage, have broad green leaves with white petioles, tightly wrapped in a cylindrical formation and usually forming a compact head. Napa cabbage is lighter in color than bok choy, which is also sometimes called Chinese cabbage. Napa cabbage is widely used in China, Japan, and Korea and is also readily found in many North American, European and Australian cities. The flavor of napa cabbage is described as delicate compared to bok choy or Western cabbage, and it can be used in stir-fry with other ingredients.

Photo 1.9 Napa cabbage.

Photo 1.10 Napa cabbage cross section.

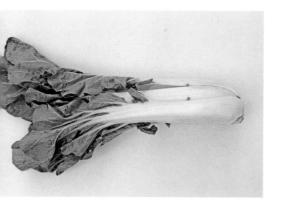

Photo 1.11 Chinese bok choy cabbage.

B. Chinese bok choy cabbage, (pak-choi), scientific name: *Brassisa rapa (Chinensis Group)*, Chinensis varieties do not form heads; instead, they have smooth, dark green leaf blades forming a cluster reminiscent of mustard or celery. Bokchoy has a mild flavor and a higher concentration of vitamin A. Both Chinese cabbage varieties are great to use in salads.

Sturdy, abundant, and inexpensive to grow, cabbage is a dietary staple widely cultivated all over the world. It stores so well that it is available throughout the year. However, it is at its best during the late fall and winter months when it is in season. Cabbage is a winter vegetable and the peak season for most cabbages runs from November through April. Fresh whole cabbage will keep in the refrigerator for one to six weeks depending on the type and variety. Hard green, white or red cabbages will keep the longest while the more delicate Savoy and Chinese varieties should be used more quickly. Fermented cabbage will easily last 6 months when kept in a cool room.

The inner leaves of the head cabbage are protected from the sunlight by the surrounding leaves and they are lighter in color. Packaged freshly shredded cabbage and carrots are available in every supermarket and need no introduction, this is a coleslaw salad. The recipe can be elaborated on and shredded red and green cabbage can be combined with fresh lemon juice, olive oil, turmeric, cumin, coriander, and black pepper to make coleslaw in Indian style.

"Cabbage is the physician of the poor"

-Dr. Blanc, 1881

Cabbage is one of the best vegetables there is. It is credited with providing the following benefits:

- Cholesterol reduction, raw, fermented or steamed cabbage only.
- Better functioning of digestive tract.
- Rich supply of vitamins and minerals.

In the past fresh and fermented cabbage were used for medicinal purposes. Fresh cabbage leaves were applied externally to wounds and infections and sauerkraut and sauerkraut juice were taken internally. It was a well known fact that drinking sauerkraut juice was an effective remedy to remove all kinds of worms (roundworms, tapeworms and others) from the system for good. Cabbage and sauerkraut are rediscovered again and there is an abundance of information on the Internet about the great benefits of a diet that includes this vegetable.

All About Sauerkraut

Sauerkraut is the German word for fermented, salted, shredded cabbage. In Poland it is known as kapusta kiszona, in Ukraine it is called kysla kapusta (кисла капуста) and in Russian kyslya kapusta (кислая капуста). The sauerkraut manufacturing process is very simple and requires only salt, cabbage and time. The fermenting temperature will affect the quality of the product. In addition to salt other ingredients are sometimes added, for example apples, juniper berries or caraway seeds. In Asian countries such as China, Japan and Korea making fermented cabbage products is an art in itself. There, fermented cabbage is mixed with other vegetables, as well as with pickled shrimp and oysters. Hot peppers are always added, a procedure that is usually not practiced in Europe. Sauerkraut was the most important vegetable in the Roman Empire and was thought to have medicinal values. Originally it was made by soaking cabbage leaves in vinegar or sour wine. In medieval times in Germany and Poland cabbage was fermented with salt, seasonings and berries. Sauerkraut made with quartered apples or sliced apples turns out particularly nice. Regardless of how it is made or called, all fermented cabbages share one factor together: they are very *healthy*. Sauerkraut is rich in vitamin C, an important fact that was known in the past. Barrels of sauerkraut were kept on ships to provide a supply of vitamin C and to prevent a nasty disease known as scurvy. Scurvy infected gums which resulted in a loss of teeth and eventual death. Between 1500 and 1800, it has been estimated that scurvy killed at least two million sailors. According to Jonathan Lamb, "In 1499, Vasco da Gama lost 116 of his crew of 170; In 1520, Magellan lost 208 out of 230; all mainly to scurvy." It has been recorded that when Captain Cook secured barrels with sauerkraut for his voyages, he did not lose one sailor to the disease. However, it was not until 1747 that James Lind formally proved that scurvy could be treated and prevented by supplementing the diet with citrus fruit such as limes or lemons.

Fermented sauerkraut is considered a probiotic, a natural ingredient that is beneficial to one's health. Probiotics contain live microorganisms thought to be healthy for the host organism. Lactic acid bacteria are present in our intestines and are responsible for digesting food. They break down food by fermentation. Homemade sauerkraut is loaded with lactic acid bacteria, so is yogurt, which is another probiotic. A fermented cabbage contains living bacteria from the *Lactobacillus* family, the same bacteria are present in our digestive tract. Whenever we ingest sauerkraut we supply an additional army of bacteria which lends a helping hand to bacteria which are already present in our stomach. Now our body gets a little break and can work less hard. Take for example a person that was very sick and accepted a heavy dose of antibiotics, or a person that has been under chemotherapy treatment. Those treatments kill all kinds of bacteria in our body, both the bad and the good ones. In such a case eating sauerkraut will speed up the rebuilding of the bacterial flora that was damaged by the medical treatments. In many German households a child had to eat sauerkraut on a weekly basis as it "was good for him."

A very important distinction must be made here, between a naturally fermented cabbage made at home and its commercially produced version. Only fermented and uncooked sauerkraut exhibits those beneficial characteristics. Cans of commercially manufactured sauerkraut are usually pasteurized (heat treated) in order to increase storage life. This process kills *Lactobacillus* beneficial bacteria and destroys some of the vitamin C, therefore such a product does not offer the same health benefits as homemade sauerkraut. The product becomes a sauerkraut flavored cabbage, but cannot be considered the probiotic anymore. What is left is just a can of fermented cabbage. Much of the commercial sauerkraut cabbage is not even fermented but only soaked in salt and vinegar to mimic the flavor of traditional sauerkraut.

The following table lists different cabbages and their nutritional values.

Nutrient	Cabbage Type (All values per 100 g serving size) Value units in grams or as noted				
	White	Red	Savoy	Chinese Napa	Chinese Bok Choy
Water	92.18	90.39	91.0	94.39	95.32
Energy	25 cal	31 cal	27 cal	16 cal	13 cal
Protein	1.28	1.43	2.00	1.20	1.50
Total fat	0.10	0.16	0.10	0.20	0.20
Ash	0.64	0.64	0.80	0.98	0.80
Carbohydrate, by difference	5.80	7.37	6.10	3.23	2.18
Fiber, total dietary	2.5	2.1	3.1	1.2	1.0
Sugars, total	3.20	3.83	2.27	1.41	1.18
Minerals					
Calcium, Ca	40 mg	45 mg	35 mg	77 mg	105 mg
Iron, Fe	0.47 mg	0.80 mg	0.40 mg	0.31 mg	0.80 mg
Magnesium, Mg	12 mg	16 mg	28 mg	13 mg	19 mg
Phosphorus, P	26 mg	30 mg	42 mg	29 mg	37 mg
Potassium, K	170 mg	243 mg	230 mg	238 mg	252 mg
Sodium, Na	18 mg	27 mg	28 mg	9 mg	65 mg
Zinc, Zn	0.18 mg	0.22 mg	0.27 mg	0.23 mg	0.19 mg
Copper, Cu	0.019 mg	0.017 mg	0.062 mg	0.036 mg	0.021 mg
Manganese, Mn	0.160 mg	0.243 mg	0.180 mg	0.190 mg	0.159 mg
Selenium, Se	0.3 µg	0.6 µg	0.9 µg	0.6 µg	0.5 µg
Vitamins					
Vitamin C	36.6 mg	57.0 mg	31.0 mg	27.0 mg	45.0 mg
Thiamin	0.061 mg	0.064 mg	0.070 mg	0.040 mg	0.040 mg
Riboflavin	0.040 mg	0.069 mg	0.030 mg	0.050 mg	0.070 mg
Niacin	0.234 mg	0.418 mg	0.300 mg	0.400 mg	0.500 mg
Pantothenic acid	0.212 mg	0.147 mg	0.187 mg	0.105 mg	0.088 mg
Vitamin B-6	0.124 mg	0.209 mg	0.190 mg	0.232 mg	0.194 mg
Folate, total	43 µg	18 µg	80 µg	79 µg	66 µg
Choline, total	10.7 mg	17.1 mg	12.3 mg	7.6 mg	6.4 mg
Betaine	0.4 mg	0.1 mg	0.5 mg	0.3 mg	0.3 mg
Vitamin A,	5 mcg_RAE	56 mcg_RAE	1000 IU	318 IU	223 mcg_RAE
Carotene, beta	42 µg	670 µg	600 µg	no data	2681 µg
Carotene, alpha	33 µg	0	0	no data	1 µg
Vitamin E	0.15 µg	0.11 µg	0.17 µg	0.12 µg	0.09 mg
Vitamin K	76.0 µg	38.2 µg	68.8 µg	42.9 µg	45.5 mg
					Source: USDA Nutrient Database

Cabbage may be grown in the summer and in the winter. The winter version is harder and greener, in the summer cabbage is softer and yellower. The winter cabbage was usually dedicated for making sauerkraut, as the fresh cabbage kept well in cool cellars. It has been determined through experience that the highest quality sauerkraut is produced at cool fermentation temperatures. Sauerkraut made in November easily lasted until May, providing a supply of vitamin C rich food. November and December was a busy time on farms as pigs were slaughtered and processed for hams and sausages in preparation for Christmas. Sauerkraut was a survival food in harsh winters of North Europe and was consumed all the time. It became a base for cabbage soup to which potatoes and other vegetables were added. Those who were fortunate to have meat would mix it with sauerkraut to make Hunter's Stew.

An experiment was performed to check the suitability of different cabbages for making sauerkraut. White, red, savoy, napa and bok-choy cabbages were shredded and mixed with 2.5% salt. Napa and bok choy were thinly cut with a knife as their soft texture made it impractical to use a slicer. The green parts were cut across and the white stems were cut into thin julienne strips.

Photo 1.12 Five types of cabbages were used.

Photo 1.13 Different sauerkrauts, 24 hrs later. From left to right: white, red, savoy, napa and bok choy. No brine was added.

Photo 1.14 White cabbage 48 hrs later.

Photo 1.15 Red cabbage 48 hrs later.

Photo 1.16 Savoy cabbage 48 hrs later.

Photo 1.17 Napa cabbage 48 hrs later.

Photo 1.18 Bok choy cabbage 48 hrs later.

Discussion: cabbages fermented for 3 weeks at around 64° F (18° C). Red cabbage was the sweetest. Chinese cabbages released more juice, due to the higher water content they possess. Keep in mind that a cabbage will be losing moisture in time so the freshly harvested cabbage should produce the largest amount of juice. All cabbages produced fine sauerkraut, although bok choy looked and tasted slightly different due to the larger proportion of white stalks the cabbage holds. All cabbages, except savoy, released juice immediately. After 24 hours the cabbages were covered with at least 1" of juice, except savoy, where juice came only to the top, however the cabbage fermented well.

Making Sauerkraut

Sauerkraut is produced by a natural fermentation of bacteria indigenous to cabbage in the presence of 2-3% salt. These bacteria are known as *Lactobacillus* lactic acid producing bacteria, they are not unique to cabbage, but can be found in pickles and meat as well. They convert sugar into lactic acid. Products such as yoghurt, sour cream, cheeses, the majority of semi-dry fermented sausages such as summer sausage, pepperoni and salamis, all of these are produced by the action of *Lactobacillus* bacteria. Many of these products require the addition of starter cultures, which are commercially grown strains of *Lactobacillus* and other bacteria types that initiate the fermentation process. However, cabbage contains such large amounts of those beneficial bacteria that a strong fermentation occurs naturally. Fermentation is nothing else but the spoilage of food. Usually such food will be discarded, however, when the process is controlled, the result is an edible and tasty product. Wine, beer, and alcoholic spirits are all made by fermentation, where *Saccharomyces* yeasts convert sugar into alcohol.

Effect of Salt

As cabbage contains 90-95% water, and from 1.18-3.83% sugar, it is a wonderful media for bacteria to grow. The amount of salt in cabbage varies from 9-65 mg (0.009-0.065%), which is too low to inhibit bacteria growth. *Lactobacillus* bacteria are beneficial bacteria and they are on our side. However, there are other bacteria also present in food: spoilage bacteria will spoil the food and the dangerous (pathogenic) bacteria may do us harm. To keep those unfriendly types at bay, we have to introduce an extra amount of salt into the cabbage. Most bacteria hate salt and their ability to grow is severely restricted. *Lactobacillus* bacteria don't like salt either, however, they can tolerate the presence of salt *better* than other types. This means that by introducing two or more percent of salt we prevent spoilage bacteria from multiplying, yet beneficial bacteria can still grow and produce lactic acid. However, if more than 3% of salt is added, the product becomes too salty and may have to be rinsed or soaked before consumption. *Lactobacillus* bacteria consume sugar and produce lactic acid and CO_2 (soda gas). Lactic acid increases the acidity of cabbage and makes it even harder for spoilage bacteria to compete. The cabbage becomes more microbiologically stable in time and fermented cabbage becomes a stable sauerkraut. The highest quality sauerkraut is obtained when 2.25-2.5% salt is mixed with shredded cabbage.

Low Salt Sauerkraut

It is possible to make sauerkraut with less salt, but more care is needed. Firstly, adding 2.5% salt results in an immediate release of juice from the cabbage. You can feel how your fist becomes submerged in brine when packing shredded cabbage. Using less salt, for example 1.2%, results in a poor juice release and the cabbage most likely will not be covered with brine and will spoil. The fix is to make a brine (1½ Tbsp of salt per quart of water) and pour it over the cabbage. This, however, beats the purpose of making a low salt sauerkraut as we end up adding salty water anyhow. Such sauerkraut will not keep long, but it may be canned.

Effect of Fermentation Temperature

The best quality sauerkraut is produced at 64-72° F (18-22° C) temperatures. *Lactobacillus* family of bacteria consists of many different strains and they all exhibit different preferences for optimal growth. Temperatures of 45.5° F (7.5° C) to 65° F (18° C) favor the growth and metabolism of *L.mesenteroides*. Temperatures higher than 72° F (22° C) favor the growth of the *Lactobacillus species*. Generally, *lower temperatures produce higher quality sauerkraut,* although at 45.5° F (7.5° C) bacteria are growing so slow that the cabbage may need 6 months to complete fermentation. Higher temperatures produce sauerkraut in 7-10 days but of lesser quality. This creates such a fast fermentation that some types of lactic acid bacteria don't grow at all and some reaction might not take place at all. The end products will exhibit a less complex flavor.

- At 45.5° F (7.5° C) fermentation time is up to 6 months.
- At 65° F (18° C) fermentation time is 3 weeks.
- At 90-96° F (32-36° F) fermentation time is 10 days.

Cabbage contains enough lactic acid bacteria in order to ferment and produce sauerkraut with salt alone. In order to obtain a product of the highest quality all those bacteria strains must ferment in a certain sequence. This happens naturally as long as sauerkraut is fermented around 68° F (20° C).

Fermentation Step by Step

The fermentation process explained below is known as a wild fermentation as no starter cultures are added. Actually, it is not common to use cultures for making sauerkraut as cabbage contains all the lactic acid producing bacteria that are needed in sufficient quantities. This natural process is known as the floral succession and is dependent by the acidity (pH) of the growth medium, which in this case is shredded cabbage immersed in brine. In the first stage coliform bacteria such as *Klebsiella* and *Enterobacter* which are ubiquitous in the air, lead the fermentation, and begin producing an acidic environment. With increased acidity, coliform bacteria become less effective but set the stage for *Leuconostoc bacteria* to colonize the medium.

1. *Leuconostoc mesenteroides* – they are the smallest and start fermentation first producing around 0.25 to 0.3% lactic acid. They are heterofermenters, this means that they produce *different* compounds such as lactic acid, acetic acid (vinegar), ethyl alcohol, carbon dioxide (soda gas) and mannitol. The last one is a bitter flavored compound which is metabolized later by *Lactobacillus plantarum*. All those acids, in combination with alcohol from aromatic esters, contribute to the characteristic flavor of high quality sauerkraut. If the temperature is higher than 72° F (22° C) they might not grow and that would be detrimental to the flavor of sauerkraut. In about 2 days *Leuconostoc mesenteroides* will produce 0.3% lactic acid and *this increased acidity will restrict its growth.* Nevertheless, the enzymes they produced will continue to develop flavor.

2. *Lactobacillus plantarum* – this strain takes over the production of lactic acid from *Leuconostoc mesenteroides* and continues fermenting until an acidity level of 1.5 to 2% is achieved. *L. plantarum* will ferment at temperatures higher than 72° F (22° C) and it can grow at higher acidity levels. It will ferment at lower temperatures as well, albeit at much slower rate. *Lactobacillus plantarum* is the most popular lactic acid bacteria strain and it ferments sauerkraut, pickles, cheese and even meat. This bacteria is

14

a homofermenter meaning that it produces one compound only. It consumes sugar and produces *lactic acid* which imparts an acidic taste to fermented food. At the end of this stage sauerkraut has an acceptable quality and can be served or canned.

3. *Lactobacillus pentoaceticus (L.brevis)* – continue fermenting until an acidity level of 2.5 – 3% is obtained. If there is enough sugar left, the fermentation will continue until all sugar supply is exhausted. Refrigeration halts the fermentation process. If left out in room temperature air for a long time, the kraut will get more acidic and sour, eventually reaching a point when it might be non edible. Any change to the above cycles of lactic acid production will alter the taste and quality of sauerkraut. As long as the proper amount of salt is added and the recommended temperatures are observed, the three bacteria strains will ferment cabbage in the proper sequence.

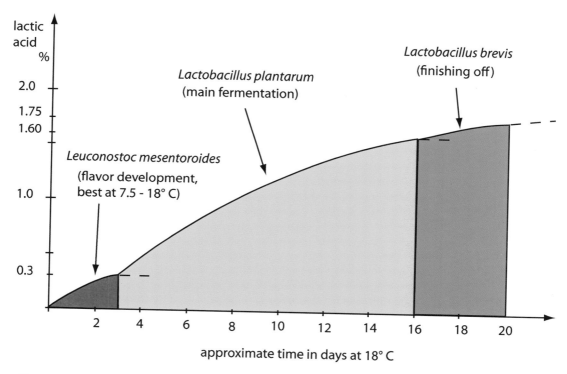

Fig. 2.1 Sauerkraut fermentation graph.

Air Removal

This is of paramount importance to exclude oxygen in all phases of the sauerkraut production process. The presence of oxygen creates favorable conditions for acid loving yeasts and mods to grow. They are not limited to sauerkraut production only, but are a nuisance during making pickles, wine or even salami. However, they need air to survive and concentrate only on the surface of the product. Traditional home production relied on periodic inspections of fermenting casks, removing any slime and washing cabbage leaves, weights and covering cloth. Today we have equipment that automatically takes care of air removal problems as explained in the Equipment chapter.

Making Sauerkraut

1. Preparation. Use fresh and sweet cabbage. A large cabbage may be halved or quartered. The core is hard, but very nutritious so it is recommended to grate it.

Photo 2.1 Save the outer leaves.

Photo 2.4 Removing core.

Photo 2.2 Halving cabbage.

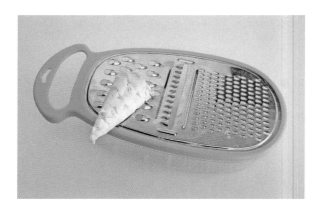

Photo 2.5 Grating core.

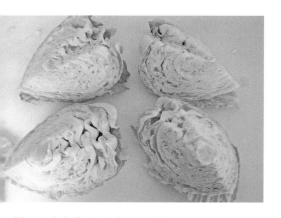

Photo 2.3 Quartering cabbage.

The composition of cabbage varies with the variety and conditions during its growth. The best cabbage for kraut are fully mature, large heads, 6 to 15 pounds, which have a solid, white interior. The larger the head, the sweeter it is. This is particularly true later in the fall after several nights of light frost. Supermarkets usually carry smaller heads, which are acceptable.

2. Shredding.

Shred cabbage very thinly, about 2 mm (1/16"), as thin slices facilitate the release of juices. These juices contain nutrients and sugar which are needed for the growth of lactic acid bacteria. When finely cut and packed in a barrel, shredded cabbage will release juice immediately. Using a mandoline slicer is helpful when processing a large quantity of cabbage, for one or two heads, a sharp knife will do.

Photo 2.6 Mandoline slicer.

Photo 2.7 Shredded cabbage.

3. Salting. Adding salt to shredded cabbage creates an osmotic pressure which results in the release of water and nutrients from the cabbage. This juice is rich in sugar, vitamins, minerals and is an excellent growth medium for bacteria involved in the fermentation. If the cabbage has been stored for a few weeks, it is somewhat dry and may release not enough brine to be fully immersed in it. If you don't see brine over the top in two days, prepare and add an extra brine. Add 25 g (4 tsp.) of salt to 950 g (1 quart) of water and pour over the shredded cabbage. Adding salt not only draws out juice but also creates hostile conditions for spoilage bacteria. Commercial producers add around 2.25%, home producers add usually between 2.25 and 2.5% salt by weight. To meet 2.5% salt requirement, 25 g (4 tsp.) of salt is added to 1 kg (2.2 lb) of cabbage.

For consistent results sauerkraut or cucumbers should be weighed. Then the weight of the sauerkraut is multiplied by the desired percentage of salt and the precise amount of salt is calculated.

Photo 2.8 General scale.

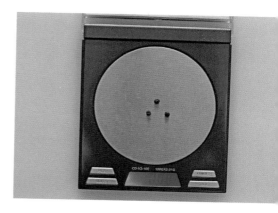

Photo 2.9 Highly accurate scale by American Weigh Scales, Inc.

Using cups, spoons or teaspoons can be misleading as for example a cup of table salt weighs differently than a cup of kosher salt. To make the matter worse an American table-spoon/teaspoon is of a different size than the European or Australian one. Use only real salt such as rock salt or sea salt, but not iodized table salt, which comes with iodine and anti-caking agents. Those extra ingredients will make the fermenting brine cloudy, which is easily noticeable with pickled cucumbers. Sea salt is great for fermentation as it contains traces of many minerals and these become nutrients for lactic acid producing bacteria. Thorough mixing of salt with cabbage is critical. Pockets of low salt distribution would result in spoilage. Pockets of very large salt concentration may result in the lack of fermentation. *Lactobacillus* are salt resistant up to a certain point and will not grow if covered with salt. The tight packing of thinly shredded cabbage will immediately squeeze cabbage juice which will mix with salt and create an equally distributed brine.

4. Packing. The salted cabbage is tightly packed into suitable containers such as clay pots, pickle crocks, glass jars or food grade plastic pails (3-5 gallons). Tight packing forces the juice out of the shredded cabbage. As the first layer of about 25 mm (one inch) of shredded sauerkraut was placed at the bottom, it was sprinkled with salt, then another layer of shredded cabbage was added and more salt added.

You can mix shredded sauerkraut with salt in a large mixing bowl and then place it in a container. If a significant amount of cabbage is shredded, the mixing and packing can be done in stages. Make sure you tamp it down very firmly using your hands or some suitable device, for example a potato masher. The advantage of packing cabbage using your hands is that we can feel how well a juice is released.

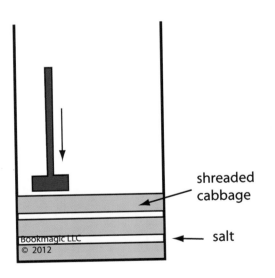

shreaded cabbage

salt

Fig. 2.2 Salting and packing cabbage.

Photo 2.10 Salting and mixing cabbage in a container allows for a uniform salt distribution.

18

The packing continues until the barrel is about three quarters full. The extra space is needed as the fermenting cabbage will expand. Mark the initial level of the packed cabbage on a glass and you will be surprised to see how much the sauerkraut will expand.

In the old days sauerkraut was packed by using young children who jumped barefoot on shredded cabbage in huge oak barrels. That procedure packed cabbage and promoted the release of juice. This should not come as a surprise because wine was made the same way. Children and young ladies used to dance on wine grapes in large wooden casks in order to release the juices.

Photo 2.11 Packing cabbage.

Illustration by Tadeusz Kasperkowicz

Photo 2.12 White cabbage 24 hours after packing.

Photo 2.13 White cabbage 72 hours after packing.

Notice how much the cabbage has expanded in volume after 72 hours.

Shredded cabbage is covered with whole cabbage leaves or a linen cloth and is weighted. The cabbage releases juice and it should be soon submerged in its own brine. The cabbage starts to ferment.

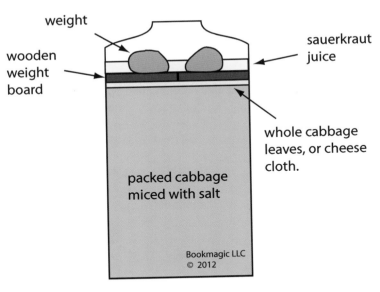

Fig. 2.3 Fermentation crock.

Photo 2.14 Shredded cabbage packed in a clay water channel crock.

Many people cover the shredded cabbage with whole cabbage leaves. If the brine gets scummy it is easier to replace cabbage leaves or a cloth than to scoop up the slime.

Photo 2.15 Less than perfect outer leaves go on top of the shredded cabbage.

Weight Plates

The purpose of the weight plate is to keep the shredded cabbage submerged in brine. Often a round wooden board was used on which a rock was usually placed. A double seal Zip-loc® plastic bag filled with salted water may be placed on top of the shredded cabbage. The bag will conform to the shape of the container, keeping shredded cabbage below the accumulating liquid. There is always a possibility that a plastic bag may break or leak out its content into the cabbage. Water will dilute the fermenting brine and may adversely affect the process, so it is wiser to fill the bag with brine. Adding 25 g (4 tsp.) of salt to 950 g (1 quart) of water makes an acceptable brine. The weight keeps the cabbage submerged in liquid and out of contact with direct air. This prevents yeasts from growing on the surface as they need oxygen to grow. Yeasts can produce slime and even discolor the sauerkraut.

Water

Fresh cabbage releases juice easily so salted water is added in very rare instances. Tap water includes chlorine to kill bacteria and will inhibit the growth of *Lactobacillus* fermenting bacteria as well. Use spring water, distilled water or boil tap water to evaporate chlorine. Needless to say only cold water should be added.

Photo 2.16 Shredded cabbage should be covered by brine.

Photo 2.17 In 24 hours plenty of brine forms and the cabbage starts to ferment.

The brine on top of the cabbage prevents yeasts and molds from producing a white scum. If any white foam accumulates in time on top of the cabbage it should be removed.

The best results are obtained when harvested vegetables are processed as soon as possible. On occasion we may end up with a drier cabbage that will refuse to release the sufficient amount of juice. If the shredded cabbage is not covered with 1" of juice within 48 hours, some salted water must be added. Add enough brine until the cabbage is 1" below water level.

Sauerkraut can be made in 10 days or six months, depending on the temperature. There is no time limit rule dictating when to eat sauerkraut. After all we eat raw cabbage when coleslaw salad is served. Sauerkraut can be eaten in a few days but the texture will still be hard. After fermentation is completed, pack sauerkraut in clean glass or food grade plastic containers. Store in a cool dark place or refrigerate. When refrigerated it will last up to a year.

Whole Cabbage Heads

Whole or half cabbage heads may be fermented in a large crock. They should be covered with finely shredded cabbage and packed tight. The process is the same as for a regular sauerkraut. The main disadvantage of open containers for making sauerkraut lies in the fact that the top surface of sauerkraut is in contact with air. We may have cabbage leaves on top and the sauerkraut may be submerged in brine, yet molds will find a way to grow on top in time. The only fix was to periodically scoop up the scum from the surface, wash out the leaves, cover and weights, and reinstall everything the way it was. If that was not performed on a regular basis, there was a danger of losing the production.

Photo 2.18 Visible slime on top of wooden plates and cabbage leaves.

Water Channel Fermenting Crocks

German Harsch fermenting crocks have been around for a long time. In the 2000's a Polish company in Boleslawiec made their presence by manufacturing high quality clay crocks. The advantage of those pots is the maintenance free operation. The same principle that enables sauerkraut water channel crocks to be so effective has been employed by wine makers for centuries. The crocks are described in detail in the Equipment section.

This sauerkraut was fermented in a Polish fermenting crock for two months and there was no trace of slime on the surface. It was checked again two months later and the result was the same, no trace of slime. After six months the sauerkraut was removed, portioned in smaller containers and placed in a refrigerator.

Photo 2.19 The fermented leaves are in a perfect shape.

Photo 2.20 Not a trace of slime after six months.

Photo 2.21 Sauerkraut juice.

Save the fermented sauerkraut juice as this is a wonderful drink. Some claim, it is a great hangover cure. It can be used as an excellent starter culture for the next production. Strain the juice and pour it into dark bottles all the way to the top to eliminate as much air as possible. This juice contains all minerals, vitamins and nutrients that lactic acid producing bacteria need to start a successful fermentation. The natural sauerkraut juice has little in common with commercial sauerkraut which in most cases contains added vinegar. This explains its unpleasant and acidic taste.

Summary of Critical Issues

- Use fresh and sweet cabbage. Cabbage should contain up to 3.5% sugar. The sweeter raw cabbage is the better sauerkraut will be obtained.

- Adding less than 2% salt might produce soft or even slimy sauerkraut. Adding less than 1% will produce sauerkraut that would be soft and unacceptable commercially. Adding more than 3.5% salt might inhibit growth of lactic acid bacteria.

- The more lactic acid that is produced the more acidic the sauerkraut becomes. There is a limit how much lactic acid can be produced as the increased acidity inhibits bacteria growth. Once the sugar supply is exhausted, lactic acid bacteria stop growing as well.

- White scum on the surface of the sauerkraut is due to yeasts and should be removed every few days. There is no reason to discard the sauerkraut.

- It is possible to use the brine from the previous sauerkraut fermentation as a starter culture for a new production. This is a common method used in the production of bread or even salami (back slopping), where part of a fermented product is saved for new production. In theory at least, it should produce a new batch with the same characteristics as the old one.

- During fermentation glucose (sugar) is converted to about 50% lactic acid, 25% acetic acid and ethyl alcohol, and 25% carbon dioxide.

- Keep the fermentation temperature below 80° F (27° C). For best quality sauerkraut maintain a fermentation temperature at around 68° F (20° C).

- The process of making sauerkraut and pickled cucumbers is very similar. Both products are made using the same equipment, cucumbers of course are not shredded, although they may be sliced.

- Keep the sufficient level of brine to cover sauerkraut.

- Fermenting glass jars should be kept in a dark place.

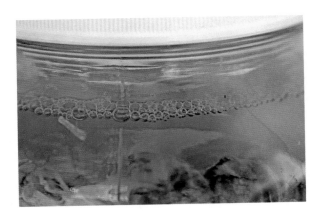

Photo 2.22 Bubbles are the sign of ongoing fermentation.

Sauerkraut Recipes

White Sauerkraut

white cabbage, 1 kg (2.2 lb)
salt, 2.25% salt, 22 g (4 tsp)
caraway seeds, 2 g (1 tsp)
whole juniper berries, 1 tsp

1. Remove outer leaves.
2. Cut cabbage in quarters, remove cores. They may be finely grated and added as well.
3. Mix cabbage with salt and spices and pack tightly in a container.
4. Cover with leaves and apply weight.
5. Ferment, preferably around 68° F (20° C), for about 3 weeks.

Red Sauerkraut

white cabbage, 1 kg (2.2 lb)
salt, 2.5% salt, 25 g (4 tsp)
apple, 2
cranberries, 1/2 cup
caraway seeds, 2 g (1 tsp)

1. Remove outer leaves.
2. Cut cabbage in quarters, remove cores. They may be finely grated and added as well. Cut apples into 6 wedges, discard stems and seeds.
3. Mix cabbage, apples, cranberries, salt and pack tightly in a container.
4. Cover with leaves and apply weight.
5. Ferment, preferably around 68° F (20° C), for about 3 weeks.

How to Can Sauerkraut

See Chapter 5 - Canning Pickles

Canning Procedure:

Packing Method	Jar Size	Process Time in Minutes at Altitudes of			
		0-1000 ft	1,001-3,000 ft	3,001-6,000 ft	Above 6,000 ft
Raw	Pints	20	25	30	35
	Quarts	25	30	35	40
Hot	Pints	10	15	15	20
	Quarts	15	20	20	25

Bigos

Bigos, also known as a Hunter's Stew, is a traditional stew typical of Polish, Lithuanian, Belarusian and Ukrainian cuisine, considered to be the Polish and Ukrainian national dish. The seasonal availability of cabbage made bigos a traditional part of the winter diet in those countries. There is no single recipe for this delicious stew of cabbage and meat, as recipes vary from region to region and from family to family. However, the main ingredients are invariably the same, what differs is the seasonings and minor details in the preparation and cooking process.

The main ingredients are:

- sauerkraut.
- fresh white cabbage.
- various cuts of meat and sausages.
- dry mushrooms, dry plums (prunes), onions and seasonings.

Seasonings: pepper, tomato paste, bay leaf, marjoram, caraway. In the past bigos was made without tomato paste as the product was not known then. You can make bigos without fresh white cabbage, but you *cannot make bigos without sauerkraut*. Adding fresh cabbage makes bigos milder.

Meats may include pork, ham, bacon, back fat, beef, veal, sausage, leftover cuts and they may be of a regular or smoked type. The richer variety of meats the better the bigos will be. Usually, an equal amount of meat is added to cabbage, so this is a very filling dish.

General Instructions:
All ingredients are mixed together and slow cooked for at least three hours. To replace lost moisture a red table wine may be added. Finished bigos should be quite thick and brown in color, there should not be any liquid on the plate when bigos is served.

Serving:
Bigos is eaten hot. It may be served with mashed potatoes or bread. As with many stews, bigos can be kept in a cool place or refrigerated and then reheated later – it is said that its flavor actually intensifies when reheated. The general consensus is that bigos tastes better when it has been frozen and reheated a few times. When reheating, it is a good idea to add a little red dry wine.

Notes:

• If no fresh cabbage is added, the sauerkraut should be well rinsed and drained, otherwise bigos may end up with a sour taste.

• Wild game meat is great with bigos.

• No hot peppers are added to bigos.

Photo 2.23 Bigos.

Bigos

Materials:

1 kg (2.2 lb) fresh cabbage
1 kg sauerkraut (2.2 lb)
500 g (1.1 lb) fat pork, bacon, spare ribs
500 g (1.1 lb) beef
500 g (1.1 lb) smoked sausage, diced
2 onions
60 g (2 oz) dry prunes
60 g (2 oz) dry mushrooms
225 g (8 oz) tomato paste

Ingredients:

salt, 6 g (1 tsp)
pepper, 4 g (2 tsp)
marjoram, 2 g (1 tsp)
allspice, 2 berries
garlic, 4 cloves
bay leaf, 2

Instructions:

1. Rinse and drain sauerkraut. Soak dry mushrooms, then cut into large pieces, save the liquid. Soak dry prunes in a little water, save the liquid.
2. Pre-cook any fresh meat in water.
3. Slice thinly white fresh cabbage, cover with a little water and slow cook for 30 minutes.
4. Cut beef and pork into smaller pieces, dice sausage and add to fresh cabbage which should be soft by now.
5. Dice onions and fry in lard or oil, until golden. Add some flour to onion and stir on little heat. Add 4 tablespoon of cold water, mix together and add to fresh cabbage. Mix together.
6. Add sauerkraut and all remaining ingredients. Add leftover liquid from mushrooms and prunes. Mix everything together.
7. Slow cook for 1 hour.

Notes:

You can replace fresh cabbage with sauerkraut.
Stirring onions in flour is optional.

Vegetarian Bigos

Materials:

white cabbage, shredded, 1 kg (2.2 lb)
sauerkraut, 1 kg (2.2 lb)
onions, 3
garlic, 3 cloves
fresh mushrooms, 28 g (1 oz)
prunes 28 g (1 oz)
tomato paste, 56 g (2 oz)
red wine, 50 ml (3 Tbsp)
soy sauce, 15 ml (1 Tbsp)
hard tofu, 225 g (8 oz)

Ingredients:
pepper, 4 g (2 tsp)
allspice, berries
juniper, 3 berries

Instructions:
1. Rinse and drain sauerkraut. Soak dry prunes in a little water, save the liquid. Slice fresh mushrooms in half.
2. Slice thinly white fresh cabbage, cover with a little water and slow cook for 30 minutes.
3. Fry in oil diced onion, diced garlic and fresh mushrooms. Add wine and soy sauce.
4. Place everything together and slow cook for 60 minutes.
5. Add diced tofu and mix together.

Cabbage Soup

This is another East European Classic, known in Poland as "kapusniak." In most cases it is made from sauerkraut, sometimes from equal parts of sauerkraut and fresh cabbage, and very seldom from fresh cabbage only. The chopped smoked meats are preferred such as smoked sausage, ham, bacon or spareribs. Spareribs, smoked or not go very well with this soup. The soup may be made without any meat at all, thus becoming a vegetarian variety. The soup relates somewhat to "bigos" but is much thinner due to the added stock.

sauerkraut, 500 g (1.10 lb)
bacon, 150 g (5 oz oz)
diced ham, sausage or pork spareribs, 150 g (5 oz)
potato, 4
carrot, 2
parsnip, 1
onions, 2
celery stalk, 1
bay leaf, 1
allspice, 4 berries
pepper, 2 g (1 tsp)

1. Place any uncooked meat in 2 liter (2 quarts) of water and cook for 30 minutes.
2. Dice or grate coarsely carrot, parsnip, celery stalk and place in water. Add bay leaf, allspice and pepper. Cook for 15 minutes.
3. Drain sauerkraut, save the juice. Cut sauerkraut into shorter lengths. Although cabbage has been previously shredded, some shreds may be too long for a soup.
4. Add sauerkraut to vegetables and slow cook for 60 minutes.
5. Peel off potatoes and dice. Boil for 15 minutes (don't overcook), then drain.
6. Dice onion finely. Dice or slice ham, sausage or bacon. Place meats in lard or oil and cook for a few minutes. Add onion and cook until glassy looking.
7. Add meats and onion to sauerkraut and cook everything together for 10 minutes.

Notes:
- Taste soup, if not sourly enough, add some sauerkraut juice.
- Don't boil potatoes in a pot with vegetables. Potatoes must be cooked separately.
- A cube of beef bouillon may be added for a stronger flavor.

Reuben Sandwich

The Reuben sandwich is a classical hot sandwich of American origin that consists of layered meat, sauerkraut and Swiss cheese, with a dressing. These are grilled between slices of pumpernickel or rye bread. The meat is usually corned beef and the dressing is either Thousand Island or Russian.

1. Toast 2 slices of rye bread and spread with butter.
2. Place on toast a slice of Swiss cheese, corned beef and sauerkraut. Apply Russian or Thousand Island dressing.
3. Place a slice of Swiss cheese on top and cover with the second toast. Cut in half.

Photo 2.24 Reuben sandwich.

Rachel sandwich

The Rachel sandwich is a variation on the standard Reuben sandwich that substitutes pastrami for the corned beef and coleslaw for the sauerkraut. Sliced turkey may be used instead of corned beef or pastrami. In some parts of the United States, especially Michigan, this turkey variant is known as a "Georgia Reuben" or "California Reuben", which sometimes uses barbecue sauce instead of Russian or Thousand Island dressing.

1. Take two slices of rye bread and butter well both sides. Toast both sides.
2. Place sliced ham, sliced turkey, Swiss cheese, sliced onions and sliced tomatoes.
3. Add coleslaw and Russian dressing.

Blue Reuben Sandwich

The Blue Reuben is a variation on the standard Reuben sandwich. Blue Cheese Dressing replaces Thousand Island or Russian.

Notes:
A slice of tomato is often added.
A vegetarian version tastes well.
A grilled Reuben tastes great.
Swiss cheese may be substituted with American or mozzarella cheese.
Subway sandwich roll nay be used for those who don't like rye bread.
Rye bread may be browned on a frying pan with a bit of oil.
Mustard is sometimes used instead of dressing.

Equipment

Sauerkraut and other vegetables can be processed using simple equipment such as a kitchen knife, food grade plastic bucket, a clay jar and a suitable weight. There is also a variety of professionally made sauerkraut fermentation crocks made from baked clay such as the German Harsch or Polish fermentation crocks.

Cabbage Slicer

It is hard to beat the efficiency of a mandoline cabbage slicer when many cabbages need to be shredded. It has been around for hundreds of years and it is one of those designs that is not easy to improve upon.

Four fingers on the cabbage, thumb behind the sliding box and the cabbage is shredded in a few moves. In order not to cut your fingers you have to stop shredding when little cabbage still remains. A new cabbage quarter is placed on those remaining leaves and the operation continues.

Photo 3.1 Mandoline slicer.

Photo 3.2 Shredding cabbage.

There is a variety of small mandoline slicers, general purpose slicers, and other gadgets available on the Internet that will shred cabbage and other vegetables very well.

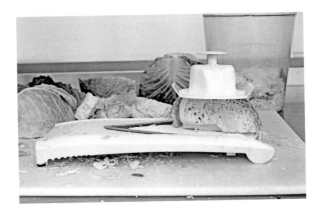

Photo 3.3 Small mandoline slicer.

Knife

If you plan on making enough sauerkraut to just meet your own or a small family's needs, you can slice cabbage with a kitchen knife, just make your cuts 1/16-1/8" thin. Keep in mind that the cabbage has to be cored and is normally cut into quarters, even if a mandoline slicer is employed. In some cases, for example when shredding Chinese soft textured cabbage, the knife is the most practical tool.

Fermentation Containers

The process of making sauerkraut is very forgiving as sauerkraut is one of those great foods that needs very little help on our part and it always turns out great. Any glass or food grade plastic container can be adapted for making a top quality fermenting vessel. The container should have a large mouth to facilitate the loading and removal of sauerkraut. Fermented containers should not be made from regular metals (stainless steel is the exception), as the fermentation produces lactic and acetic acid, which will react with metal. There are two types of containers:

- Open container.
- Closed container.

Plastic buckets make wonderful open type fermenting crocks as:

- They can be obtained for free.
- They have large capacity. Five gallons (19 liters) is a huge container.
- A plate and a weight can be be placed on top.

Photo 3.4 Supermarkets get their foods delivered in such buckets. Their capacity is usually 3-5 gallons.

Photo 3.5 If you are not sure of the origin of the bucket, you may line it with a plastic cooking bag.

Photo 3.6 Those buckets have an inside diameter of 11.25" (28.5 cm) and a large dinner plate fits on top perfectly.

Glass jars

Glass jars are great solutions for people who want to make 1-2 gallons of product or who want to try out different recipes or ideas.

Photo 3.7 Fermenting glass jar.

Photo 3.8 Fermenting glass jar.

Photo 3.9 Fermenting glass jar.

The glass jars shine in their usefulness as an educational tool. When shredded cabbage is placed in a glass jar, it can be almost immediately observed whether cabbage releases juice and how much. This can be noted on a daily basis and some corrective steps may be taken where needed. On the other hand not much can be learned from staring at the clay crock. When a cabbage is dumped into a clay container, the cover must be lifted to check the status of the fermentation. There is not much to be seen anyhow, as the weight plates are lying on the top of the cabbage and the inside is dark. The amount of released brine, the beginning of slime (if any), all that can be only roughly estimated. However, in the case of a glass jar, it is like watching fish in an aquarium, it is a live ongoing show which helps us understand the process better.

Mark the initial level of the packed cabbage on the glass, then you will be surprised to see how much the sauerkraut will expand. Needless to say, pack it up to about 3/4 of the container. During fermentation, the movement of gas and air bubbles can be easily observed through the glass. A one gallon capacity glass jar will easily hold 6.6 lb (3 kg) shredded cabbage, even if filled only to 3/4 of its volume. A wide mouth opening is preferable as it allows for easy placement of a weight.

Weights

Sauerkraut or pickles should be submerged in brine in order to create a barrier between the product and the air above. This prevents yeasts and mold from having access to the air. Originally wooden covers were placed on top of the fermenting product and the additional weight was placed on top. Rocks and bricks were often used. When a wide mouth clay, glass or plastic jar is used, the weight can be *almost* as wide as the mouth. Include 1/4" clearance for one piece wood weights as they have a tendency to warp when wet. Such a tightly fitting weight may get jammed inside the jar making removal impossible.

Photo 3.10 Sauerkraut weight split plate. When the mouth of a crock is narrower than its body, a split weight must be used.

Photo 3.11 Sauerkraut weight plate. Inverted glass plate used as a cover. A saucer filled with water or a large gravel stone can supply the weight.

Photo 3.12 For a straight jar a one piece weight plate is the best solution. The holes allow the gas to escape and enable easy plate removal.

Photo 3.13 Double zipper Ziploc® bags come in different sizes and when filled with brine make a great weight.

Clay Fermenting Crocks

Commercially produced fermenting crocks are usually made from baked clay.

Photo 3.14 American open clay fermenting crocks come in different sizes. However, fermenting cabbage in open crocks still requires periodic vigil for any signs of spoilage.

Photo 3.5 Water channel clay fermenting crocks. Polish Boleslawice crock on the left, German Harsch on the right. They come in sizes from 5-50 liters (1.3-13.25 gal).

Photo 3.16 Fermenting crock, lid and weights.

Photo 3.17 After packing sauerkraut, the channel is filled with water.

Photo 3.18 The lid is placed in water on top of the water channel.

The Water Channel Fermenting Crock Principle

The principle is based on water separating the inside of the vessel from the outside air. It has been used for centuries in wine fermentation where a simple, inexpensive tube of glass known as an "air lock" performed the trick.

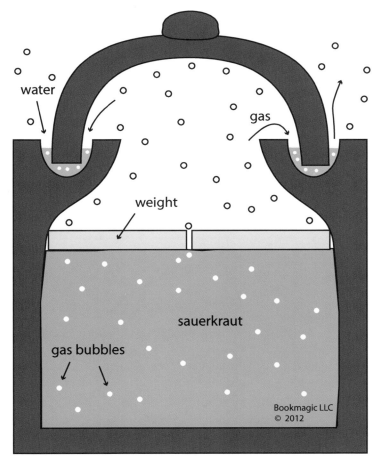

Fig. 3.1 Water channel clay fermenting crock is a maintenance free device as long as the water is present in a channel. This crock produces a top quality product. Water of course evaporates, so it must be added when needed.

The main advantage of German and Polish fermenting crocks is that the water channel creates a barrier between the product and the outside air. Carbon dioxide gas (soda gas) is created during fermentation and it pressurizes the inside of the crock. Carbon dioxide and air escape from the crock through the water channel. The outside air is at a lower pressure and cannot get inside the crock. As a result there is no air available to any yeasts or molds that might be inside and there is no white foam on top of the product. The lid is not removed during fermentation and only water is periodically added to the water channel. We have kept sauerkraut undisturbed for 3 months after fermentation stopped and the quality was superb. If a crock is left unattended for long time and all channel water evaporates away, the advantage of the design is gone as the outside air will sip in. Clay fermented crocks come with split clay weights.

Making Your Own Fermenting Containers

The factory made clay containers are very expensive. One can make his own container at a fraction of the cost, yet it will perform as well as the commercially made models. A simple yet practical version of a fermenting crock is a glass (or food grade plastic) jar that has a double bubble air lock attached to the lid. This is the same set up that is used for making wine in five gallon glass carboys. Shredded cabbage is tightly packed, weighted and the lid is secured on. When cabbage is fermenting the bubbles are travelling through the air-lock. A hole is drilled in the lid and a rubber stopper is placed in the hole. Then the air lock is inserted into the stopper (it has a hole) and a tight fit is obtained. Accumulating carbon dioxide gas escapes through the air lock pushing air out at the same time. After a while there is no air available to any yeasts or molds that might be inside and they cannot create the white slime on top of the product. The lid is not removed during fermentation and when the bubbles stop, the fermentation is completed.

Photo 3.19 Glass jar with airlock inserted into a rubber stopper.

Photo 3.20 Glass jar with airlock inserted into a rubber stopper.

Airlock Principle

The airlock is an absolutely wonderful device. It has been instrumental in making wine for centuries. It is made from plastic, costs about one dollar and it works perfectly. So what is an airlock?

An airlock is a small amount of water that physically separates the inside of a fermenting vessel from the outside air. The air creates problems during fermentation as it promotes mold development. Decomposing cabbage contains nutrients and water that bacteria and molds consume, but molds need the air to survive. Cut off the air supply and you will kill the molds. Kill the molds and the sauerkraut will be perfect every time.

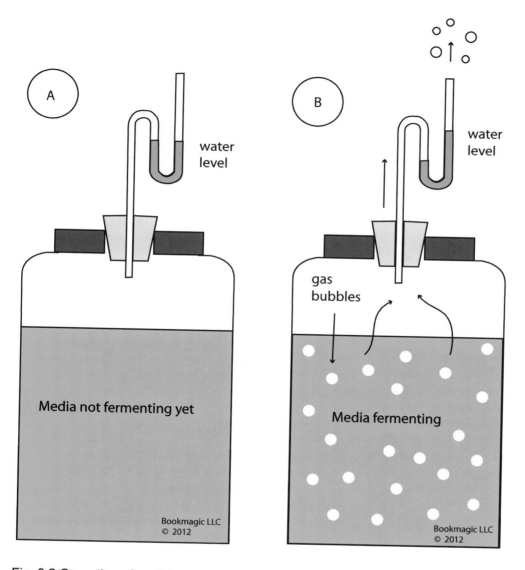

Fig. 3.2 Operation of an S-type airlock.

Drawing A - There is no fermentation taking place when freshly cut sauerkraut or fruit are placed inside of a crock. The pressure inside the crock equals the pressure on the outside of the vessel. We have an equilibrium state. This is demonstrated by the same water on both sides of the U-tube, which in our case is a part of the air-lock.

Drawing B - Bacteria need some time, usually a few hours to spring into action. They break sugar into lactic acid and produce CO_2 gas. As the gas volume increases it produces higher pressure inside of a crock. This gas travels up the tube and pushes the water level up as can be seen in a U-tube. The beauty of design lies in the fact that this travelling gas pushes out any air that resides above sauerkraut. Thus, the raising bubbles which can be seen in the U-tube are a mixture of air and CO_2, which is a soda gas. After a while there is no more air present and only gas escapes away. The absence of air depletes yeasts from growing and becoming slime on the surface.

The vessel is pressurized and the lower pressure outside air can not enter the air-lock and the crock. Even when the fermentation stops, the outside air can not travel through the water in the air-lock. Of course removing the lid equalizes the pressure on both sides, but if the fermentation is still ongoing, this air will be pushed out again. For those reasons the lid should not be removed when the fermentation is still in progress. When this operation must be performed, it is advisable to repack sauerkraut into smaller containers and keep them in a refrigerator.

Professionally made glass jars with the air-lock installed in the lid are inexpensive and available on the Internet, bur you can make your own even cheaper using basic skills and tools. In open containers a periodic inspection is needed to check for odors and to remove any slime. This requires washing weights, scooping up the slime, discarding bad top leaves or washing/replacing top cloth. With the water channel container those chores are eliminated providing that the water level in the channel is maintained. This requires adding water every few days, depending on the ambient temperature and humidity. *There is nothing to add or maintain when a glass jar with an air lock is employed.* The water will remain in its small diameter tube for months.

Airlocks come with a cap that has a number of tiny holes in it to allow gas to escape. If you lose one secure a strip of paper towel or a cloth over the top of the airlock. This prevent insects from getting in which are especially attracted to wine. They will drown first and will never make it to the container, but the sight of flies floating inside of the airlock is not appealing.

Photo 3.21 Airlock cover. Here a piece of paper towel protects the airlock from outside interference.

Wonderful Rubber Grommet

There is a little rubber grommet that costs about seven cents wholesale (package of 50) or 50 cents online. It will make a top quality fermenting vessel out of any glass jar or a food grade plastic container as long as they have a watertight cover, which most of them do. This grommet fits the airlock so you can attach the airlock to any plastic or metal lid. The grommet creates an airtight seal that is formed around the base of the airlock.

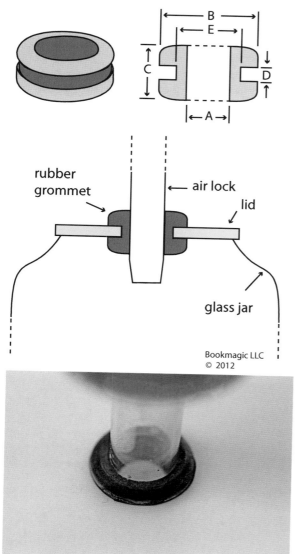

Fig. 3.3 Rubber grommet.
A - inside diameter
B - outside diameter
C - overall thickness
D - panel thickness
E - panel hole diameter

Fig. 3.4 Grommet-air-lock-jar.
Add some water to fully assembled jar, flip over and check for leaks.

Photo 3.22 Wood spade bit.

A regular metal drill bit may crack the plastic cover, so use a wood spade bit for a clean cut. First, remove the soft plastic lining from inside the cover, then drill the cover. Then make a hole in the lining using a sharp copper tubing like the one on the photo, punch it out, or cut the hole out with a knife. Re-insert the lining and push in the grommet.

Photo 3.23 Grommet in the lid.

The American airlocks have an outside diameter of the stem of about 7/16" (11 mm), so for a 1 gallon glass jar the following grommet fits well: A-3/8", B-5/8", C-1/4", D-1/16", E-1/2". Grainger part #: 3MPL3.

For a 3-5 gallon plastic bucket, a grommet with a larger panel thickness "D" (3/32") is needed due to a thicker lid. Grainger part #: 3MPP9.

Note: order a few extra plastic lids, in case you damage one during drilling.

Airlock types

There are two types of airlocks:

- S-types. The pressure differential is more apparent with an S-type airlock so it is easier and faster to notice activity. This may be more important for someone brewing beer.
- 3-piece type. This type is about 2" shorter and much easier to clean.

Both airlocks are manufactured differently: the 3-piece is perfectly round, you may get a S-type that is slightly flat instead of round and won't seal well in the stopper. We use both types and never had an issue. We generally use the S-type for making wine and 3-piece for fermenting vegetables.

Note: you will notice the red liquid in our airlocks. For demonstration purposes a drop of USDA approved red food color was injected into the water. As long as the airlock is not overfilled, the colored water cannot enter the jar.

Scales

Using scales for weighing vegetables and salt is encouraged as it provides consistent results and does not lock us to any particular recipe. The size or the number of cabbages becomes irrelevant. For example we have 1.37 kg of a cabbage and we want to use 2% salt: 1370 x 0.02 = 27.4 g of salt, regardless whether we add table salt, sea salt or Kosher salt. It is impossible to come up with such a precise amount when using spoons as a unit of measure.

Photo 3.24 Scales.

Japanese Pickle Press

The Japanese pickle press also known as a Tsukemono press, is a user friendly container for making fermented vegetables. Unlike water channel crocks or airlock glass jars, *it is not watertight* so a periodic inspection for any accumulation of slime must be performed. However, no weights are necessary as the necessary pressure is generated by turning a screw and clamping down onto the pickles. The cover can be unlocked in a second, fermented vegetable removed, then the cover is reinstalled and the pressure re-applied again.

The photos below depict white daikon radishes which were thinly sliced, mixed with 2% salt. In 6 hours there was 1" inch of brine covering radishes.

Photo 3.25 Sliced daikon radish.

The Japanese pickle press may be the best introduction for learning the art of fermenting vegetables. It is easy to operate, easy to clean, does not require cabbage leaves or linen cloth on top and allows visual observation of the fermentation process. The presses come in different sizes in rectangular or round shapes.

Photo 3.26 Tsukemono 3 liter pickle press is big enough to process 2 kg (4.4 lb) of vegetables.

Brine

Using brine tester, also known as salinometer or salometer, is the most accurate method of preparing brine. When there is no salt present in water the tester sinks to "0" degrees, with maximum salt added, it raises to 100 degrees. The distance between those two points is divided into 100 divisions and a very accurate scale is obtained. At 60° F, the brine is fully saturated when 26.395% salt has been added to 1 gallon (3.8 liter) of water. Adding more salt is pointless, as it will only settle down at the bottom.

Photo 3.27 The advantage of using a tester is that there is no need to measure water. Just add salt, mix and read the scale.

Photo 3.28 The brine is ready when the desired reading is obtained.

Brine Tables and How to Use Them

Adding salt to water and checking the reading with a salinometer is one method, but you can make brine much faster by using tables, the way professionals do. For example we want a 22 degrees brine to cure chicken. If you follow the 22 degree row to the right of the table you will see in Column 3 that 0.513 lb. of salt has to be added to 1 gallon of water to make 22 degree brine. To make 80 degree brine we need to mix 2.229 lb of salt with 1 gallon of water. Then check it with your salinometer and you can add a cup of water or a tablespoon of salt to get a perfect reading.

If you end up with not enough brine, make some more. If you think you may need just 1/2 gallon of 80 degree brine, take 1/2 gallon of water and add 1/2 of salt that the table asks for. In this case looking at 80 degree brine (Column 1), going to the right you can see that in Column 3 the amount of the salt needed is 2.229 lb. Yes, but this amount is added to 1 gallon of water to create 80 degree brine. Because we use only 1/2 gallon now, this amount of salt needs to be halved: 2.229 lb/2 = 1.11 lb. In other words if we add 1.11 lb. of salt to 1/2 gallon of water we will also create 80 degree brine. If you come across a recipe and you would like to determine what is the strength of the brine, just follow the two steps:

1. Find the percent of salt by weight in the solution: weight of salt/(weight of salt plus weight of water), then multiply the result by 100%.

2. Look up the tables and find the corresponding salometer degree.

For example let's find the strength of the brine that is mentioned in many recipes and calls for adding 1 pound of salt to 1 gallon of water (8.33 pounds).% salt by weight = 1lb. of salt/1 lb of salt + 8.33 lbs. (1 gallon) of water = 0.1071

0.1071 x 100 % = 10.71 % of salt

Looking in the table at Column 2 (percent salt by weight) we can see that 10.71% corresponds to 40 ½ degrees.

Another popular brine is made by adding 3/4 cup of salt (216 g) to 1 gallon (3.8 liters) of water:

216 g / 216 + 3800 g = 0.05
0.05 x 100 = 5% of salt

Looking in the table at Column 2 (percent salt by weight) we can see that 5% corresponds to 19 degrees.

- Seawater contains approximately 3.695% of salt which corresponds to 14 degrees salometer.
- At 100 degrees brine is fully saturated and contains 26.395% of salt.
- 1 US gallon of water weighs 8.33 lbs.
- 1 US gallon = 3.8 liters = 3.8 kilograms.
- Half sour cucumbers are usually made with a mild 12-20° brine and are ready to eat in 3-4 days.

The length of brining time depends on the brine strength. You can brine cabbage for 3 hours using 70° brine, or you can leave it overnight in 20° brine. Using a shorter time and stronger brine will result in a smaller loss of cabbage juice.

The readings in the table denoted in cups or spoons are based on a common table salt:

1 cup = 288 g
1 Tbsp = 18 g
1 tsp = 6 g

Kosher salt is less dense and cannot be used in those calculations. The only way to get the right readings is to weigh the salt.

Sodium Chloride (Salt) Brine Tables For Brine at 60° F (15° C)

Salometer Degrees	% of Salt by Weight	Pounds of Salt per US Gallon of Water	Grams of Salt per Quart of Water	Tablespoons of Salt per Quart
0	0.000	0.000	0.000	0.000
5	1.320	0.111	12.50	¾
10	2.640	0.226 (⅓ cup)	23.98	1⅓
11	2.903	0.249	28.25	1 ½
12	3.167	0.272	30.75	1 ¾
13	3.431	0.296	33.50	1 ¾
14	3.695	0.320 (½ cup)	36.00	2
15	3.959	0.343	38.75	2
16	4.223	0.367	41.50	2⅓
17	4.487	0.391	44.25	2½
18	4.751	0.415 (⅔ cup)	48.00	2½
19	5.015	0.440	50.00	2¾
20	5.279	0.464 (¾ cup)	54.00	3
21	5.543	0.489	55.50	3
22 ·	5.807	0.513	58.25	3 ⅓
25	6.599	0.588	66.75	3 ¾
27	7.127	0.639 (1 cup)	72.00	4
30	7.919	0.716	81.25	4 ½
35	9.238	0.848	96.00	5 ⅓
40	10.588	0.983	111.50	6
41	10.822	1.011	114.50	6 ⅓
45	11.878	1.123	127.25	7
50	13.198	1.266	143.50 (½ cup)	8
55	14.517	1.414	160.25	9
60	15.837	1.567	177	10
65	17.157	1.725	195.50	11
70	18.477	1.887	214.00	11 ¾
71	18.740	1.921 (3 cup)	216	12
80	21.116	2.229	252.75	14
85	22.436	2.409 (3.8 cup)	273.00	15
95	25.075	2.787	316.00	17 ½
100	26.395	2.986 (4.7 cup)	338.50	18 ¾

There is another set of brine tables for UK Gallons (UK imperial gallon = 4.54 liters) and it can be looked up on Internet.

Baumé scale - you may come across a scale in Baumé degrees that is based on the specific gravity of the brine measured with a hydrometer.

This chapter has covered in detail equipment that may be used for fermenting vegetables and the reader should be able to choose the container that will suit him best.

Kimchi & Tsukemono

Kimchi is a traditional fermented Korean dish made of cabbage with varied vegetables and seasonings. The main ingredients are: *Chinese cabbage, white radish, green onions, ginger, garlic and hot peppers.*

These nutritious vegetables are mixed and allowed to ferment in order to create what we call kimchi. Kimchi is also an ingredient for many other dishes where pickled baby shrimp, oysters or salted fish sauce may be added. Several types of kimchi exists, including regional and seasonal variations. It is believed that the name kimchi originated from shimchae (salting of vegetable). The Korean people absolutely love this side dish with rice, which is well known for its spicy flavor. Some of the foods made with kimchi include: kimchi-jjigae (stew), kimchi-guk (soup), kimchi-jeon (a Korean-style pancake), and kimchi fried rice. These days kimchi has been incorporated into Western style foods such as hamburgers and pizza, which are loved by many.

As cabbage is basically a winter vegetable, the greatest varieties of kimchi were prepared during the early winter. November and December are traditionally when people begin to make kimchi; women often gather together in each others homes to help with winter kimchi preparations. Korean immigrants to China, Russia, Hawaii and Japan first introduced kimchi abroad, and have continued to eat kimchi as a side dish. It gradually gained popularity even among foreigners. Accordingly, kimchi may be found wherever Koreans live. In America packaged kimchi is easily available in major supermarkets. In the past, the production and consumption of kimchi was confined to Korean societies, however, in recent years it has become a globally recognized food.

Kimchi and Hot Red Pepper

As a kind of pickled vegetable, kimchi was born in Korea around the 7th century. Many years ago, kimchi was simply regarded as a salted vegetable. Early kimchi was made of cabbage and beef stock only. Red chili, a New World vegetable not found in Korea before European contact with the Americas, was introduced to Korea from Japan after the Hideyoshi Invasions (1592-1598) and became a staple ingredient in kimchi.

Red chili pepper flakes are now used as a main ingredient for spice and a source of heat for many varieties of kimchi. This also accounts for the reddish color of kimchi. Kimchi as we know it today has retained the same qualities and cooking preparations that prevailed ever since it was first introduced centuries ago. Kimchi is a much more elaborate dish than European sauerkraut, which even today is basically fermented shredded cabbage with added salt. Most Europeans do not fancy adding red hot peppers into sauerkraut. At the beginning of the winter season a traditional Korean farm family would process one or two hundred cabbage heads for making kimchi. Kimchi was stored in the ground in large jars which were covered with a straw cushion and kept in a designated storage area. Nowadays, vegetables can be grown throughout the year in green houses so there is less need to process huge quantities of kimchi at one time. The storage is is often accomplished in modern kimchi refrigerators that offer precise temperature controls. Such an appliance is designed specifically to meet storage requirements of various kimchi types, including temperature control and different fermentation processes. In consumer surveys aimed at Korean housewives, the kimchi refrigerator ranks first always on top of the list as the most wanted household appliance. They are also great for storing wine, vegetables, fruits, meat, fish and other foods because these refrigerators are designed to offer a constant-temperature environment so that you can store foods fresh much longer than ordinary refrigerators. They can also be used as freezers.

Kimchi's Benefits

Kimchi like its Western counterpart sauerkraut are probiotics. This is due to the presence of lactic acid bacteria that produce lactic acid. Resulting lactic acid in kimchi restrains the growth of harmful bacteria in the intestines and helps relieve intestinal disorders. Kimchi is also credited for preventing adult diseases such as obesity, diabetes, and even gastrointestinal cancers. Juices from the vegetables and salt in kimchi help the intestines remain clean as well.

Korea has been officially credited with preventing SARS disease. Recently, SARS influence has struck many places throughout Asia. Severe acute respiratory syndrome (SARS) is a serious form of pneumonia. It is caused by a virus that was first identified in 2003. Infection with the SARS virus causes acute respiratory distress (severe breathing difficulty) and sometimes death. Korea has managed to stay SARS-free and some are saying that the reason for this can be found in kimchi.

Photo 4.1 Kimchi.

Photo 4.2 Kimchi.

46

The Making of Kimchi

At the first glance, making Kimchi seems to be a very complicated process which is even compounded by the variety of materials that are used. On the other hand it is easier to come up with a recipe, as there are so many of them as each region in Korea has its own. There are so many vegetables and ingredients that go into Kimchi, that it may be more correct to think of Kimchi as a Korean way of preparing vegetables and not as of a particular dish.

Some Kimchi are feremented for 2 weeks, some for 3 days, and some are consumed the moment they have been made. Some are thick and some are watery that look like a soup. Most Kimchis are made with Chinese cabbage, however, this is not set in stone and many are made without it. They can be made with white radish or turnip only. Filler materials vary as well, pickled baby shrimp, fresh shrimp, fresh oysters, squid, different types of mushrooms, Korean pear, seaweed, nuts, the list is endless. That offers a lot of freedom to a cook, who can let his imagination run wild, improvising and creating new Kimchis. However, certain ingredients such as *garlic, ginger, scallions, and red pepper flakes* or powder are nearly always added. However, there is a white kimchi, which does not include red peppers.

Kimchi can be made from 1/2 cabbage, 1/4 cabbage or the cabbage can be sliced across. Half cabbage is usually stuffed with filling and the leaves must be softened up first, which is accomplished by soaking the cabbage in brine. The process of making whole cabbage Kimchi can be divided into a few phases:

1. Preparing cabbage and slicing materials.
2. Making coloring paste and painting vegetables.
3. Stuffing cabbage.

Photo 4.3 Cutting through the root.

1. Chinese cabbage is cut in a peculiar way. Discard any poor quality outer leaves and cut off as much of the root as possible. Save better leaves for later. Cut through the bottom of the cabbage to the half-way point, then split the head into separate halves. This cutting method preserves the texture of the internal leaves.

Most kimchis are consumed in a few days so the cabbage needs to be softened, what is accomplished by salting it and placing aside for one night. The following day the cabbage is rinsed well and the excess water is drained away. Another faster method is to immerse cabbage for 3-4 hours in a brine that is made by dissolving 3 cups of salt (864 g) in 4 quarts

Photo 4.4 Splitting cabbage.

(~ 4 liters) of water. This makes 70° SAL (salometer reading) brine, which is quite strong. Making a weaker brine will increase the brining time and the cabbage will release too many valuable nutrients into the brine. The purpose of brining cabbage is to make it soft and pliable and not to make it salty. Salt will be added during mixing ingredients.

Photo 4.5 Immersing cabbage in brine.

Photo 4.6 Rinsing cabbage.

Photo 4.7 Draining water.

2. Korean red pepper powder is very mild comparing to fiercely hot cayenne peppers. You can add 0.75 ounce (21 g) to 1 kg (2.2 lb) of cabbage. Make paste by mixing red pepper powder with a small amount of water. You can soak pepper in the salted anchovy or shrimp juice, this will add an extra flavor. Coat white radish strips with red pepper paste, then add all other vegetables, salt and ingredients such as shrimp or oysters. Mix everything together. This is the stuffing.

Photo 4.8 Making red pepper paste.

Photo 4.9 Radishes are usually cut into 2" long thin julienne strips.

Photo 4.10 Coating radishes.

Photo 4.11 Mixing all together.

3. The cabbage is ready for stuffing. The filling is evenly placed between each leaf of cabbage. In order to keep all of the filling securely in the cabbage, the entire cabbage is wrapped with an outermost leaf and allowed to ferment for about 3-7 days.

Photo 4.12 While holding back the leaves, place the filling between the leaves.

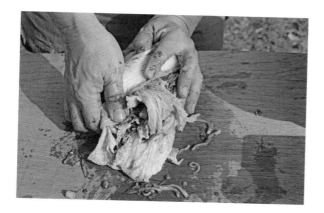

Photo 4.13 Wrap the middle of the cabbage with the outer leaves. This protects the stuffing from falling out.

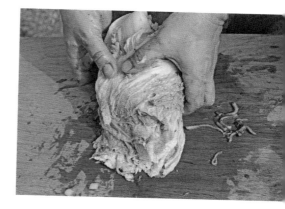

Photo 4.14 Stuffed cabbages.

Stack stuffed cabbages in a suitable container. Try to avoid any large pockets of air. Salt the outer leaves which were removed earlier and cover the stuffed cabbage. Add any residual juice and brine that may remain over. Press hard on cabbages to release any trapped air, sprinkle salt over the cabbage leaves and place a weight on top. Napa cabbage is a great juice producer so the next day the cabbage should be immersed in brine.

Photo 4.15 Stuffed cabbages in a glass jar.

Photo 4.16 - right. Stuffed cabbages in a glass jar, 24 hours later. Note the amount of brine.

Easy Kimchi

napa cabbage, 2.5 kg (5.5 lb)
scallions, 1 bunch , 250 g (8 oz)
garlic cloves, 6, crushed
ginger root, 1, finely diced, 25 g (1 oz)
red pepper powder, 1/2 cup, 40 g (1.4 oz)
salt, 50 g, (3 Tbsp)
sugar, 15 g (1 Tbsp)

1. Trim off outer leaves, split cabbage into separate halves.
2. Make a brine: 3 cups salt to 4 quarts water. Brine the cabbage for 3 hours. Rinse cabbage in fresh water and squeeze the water out, repeat twice more. Drain cabbage for 30 minutes.
3. Cut cabbage into 2" (5 cm) sections.
4. Add a little water to red pepper powder and make paste.
5. Cut scallions diagonally, dice ginger and crush garlic.
6. Add salt and sugar and mix all together.
7. Pack stuffed cabbage in a container. Put on top outer leaves that were removed in step #1. Sprinkle with salt. Place weight on top. Ferment 3 days.

Whole Cabbage Kimchi

napa cabbage, 2.5 kg (5.5 lb)
white radish, 500 g (1.76 lb)
scallions, 1 bunch , 250 g (8 oz)
garlic cloves, 6, crushed
ginger root, 1, finely diced, 25 g (1 oz)
red pepper powder, 1/2 cup, 40 g (1.4 oz)
watercress, 1 bundle, 150 g (5 oz)
pickled baby shrimp, 1/2 cup, 56 g (2 oz)
salt, 50 g, (3 Tbsp)

1. Trim off outer leaves, cut the root, and split cabbage into separate halves.
2. Make a brine: 3 cups salt to 4 quarts water. Brine the cabbage for 3 hours. Rinse cabbage in fresh water and squeeze the water out, repeat twice more. Drain cabbage for 30 minutes.
3. Make red pepper paste. Cut radishes thinly into 1" (5 cm) long julienne strips. Coat strips with the paste.
4. Cut scallions diagonally, dice ginger and crush garlic. Drain pickled baby shrimp.
5. Mix all together.
6. Pack the stuffing between the leaves. Wrap the stuffed cabbage with the outer layer of leaves.
7. Pack stuffed cabbage in a container. Put on top outer leaves that were removed in step #1. Sprinkle with salt. Place weight on top. Ferment 3 days.

Kimchi Soup

A sauerkraut soup is a popular dish in all cabbage loving countries. In East Europe it is known as "kapusniak," in Korea it is called kimchi soup.

napa cabbage, 1 kg (2.2 lb)
pork, 225 g (8 oz)
soy sauce, 45 g (3 Tbsp)
sesame oil, 42 g (3 Tbsp)
scallion, 1 bunch
red pepper powder, 30 g (1 oz)
beef broth, 1 cube

1. Dice pork or cut into strips. Marinate with sesame oil, soy sauce, and diced garlic for a few hours.
2. Cut slightly fermented (2-3 days) cabbage into 2 " (5 cm) pieces. Cut scallions diagonally.
3. Make paste: red pepper powder, finely chopped garlic and ginger.
4. Dissolve a cube of beef broth in water and apply heat. Add all ingredients and bring the mixture to a boil.
5. Slow cook for 30 minutes and serve hot.

Carrot Kimchi

napa cabbage, 2.5 kg (5.5 lb)
scallions, 1 bunch , 250 g (8 oz)
carrots, 453 g (1 lb)
garlic cloves, 6, sliced in half
ginger, finely diced, 25 g (1 oz)
red pepper powder, 1/2 cup, 40 g (1.4 oz)

1. Trim off outer leaves, split cabbage into quarters, then cut into 1" (2.5 cm) slices. Slice carrot into 1/4" (5 mm) slices.
2. Make a brine: 3 cups salt to 4 quarts water. Brine the cabbage and carrots for 3 hours. Remove cabbage and carrots, save the brine. Rinse in fresh water, drain, repeat twice more. Drain cabbage for 30 minutes.
3. Cut scallions diagonally into 1" (2.5 cm) pieces.
4. Finely dice ginger and mix with red pepper powder.
5. Mix all together.
6. Pack the mixture in a container. Put on top outer leaves that were removed in step #1. Sprinkle with salt. Place weight on top. Add enough leftover brine to submerge the mixture. Ferment 3 days.

Photo 4. Carrot kimchi.

Tsukemono

Japanese Tsukemono, or pickled vegetables, covers a wide range of prepared dishes, from slightly fermented cabbage and radishes to garlic marinated in honey. The most common kinds of tsukemono are pickled in salt or brine and they are usually served with rice. Takuan (daikon), umeboshi (ume plum), turnip, cucumber, and Chinese cabbage are among the favorites to be eaten with rice as an accompaniment to a meal. Beni shoga (red ginger) is used as a garnish on okonomiyaki, takoyaki and yakisoba. Gari (ginger) is used between dishes of sushi to cleanse the palate. Rakkyōzuke (a type of onion) is often served with Japanese curry. Kombu (seaweed, kelp) is often added. Soy sauce, miso, vinegar, rice bran (nuka), and sake lees (sake kasu), mirin (sweet rice wine) are commonly added for pickling.

Miso is a traditional Japanese seasoning produced by fermenting soybeans with salt and yeast mold known as "koji." It can also be produced from rice, barley or wheat. After fermentation time, ranging from weeks to years, the fermented ingredients are ground into a thick paste similar in texture to peanut butter. Miso is used for sauces and spreads, pickling vegetables or meats, and mixing with dashi soup stock to serve as miso soup called misoshiru, a Japanese culinary staple. Miso ranges in color from white to brown. The lighter varieties are less salty and more mellow in flavor.

Garlic in Miso

fresh garlic, 225 g (8 oz)
miso, 225 g, (8 oz)
mirin (sweet rice wine), 15 ml (1 Tbsp)

1. Peel off garlic cloves.
2. Mix miso with wine to make a paste.
3. Place some of the miso mixture in a jar, then add garlic.
4. Cover garlic with a new layer of miso.
5. Repeat the procedure until all garlic cloves are covered with miso.
6. Close the jar and refrigerate.

Photo 4.18 Making paste.

Photo 4.19 Filling jar with garlic.

Photo 4.20 Garlic in miso.

Salted Japanese Cabbage

napa cabbage, 2 kg
salt, 3%, 60 g
1 small lemon
15 cm (6 inches) dried Japanese kombu
3 hot peppers (Tabasco strength)

1. Remove 2-3 outer cabbage leaves for later use. Cut the cabbage half way from the base to the middle.
2. Tear the rest apart.
3. Split each half into quarters.
4. Sprinkle little salt into the bottom of a container.
5. Place cabbage quarters, cut sides up. Sprinkle more salt on cut cabbage, add lemon slices, kombu, and whole hot peppers.
6. Repeat until all cabbage is firmly packed. Sprinkle with remaining salt.
7. Place a lid or inverted dinner plate on top of cabbage, then add weight on top.
8. There should be liquid over the plate the next day. Ready to eat in 3 days.

Photo 4.21 Dried Japanese kombu can be cut into smaller squares.

Chessboard Radish

Photo 4.22 Stuffed radish.

large diameter white radish, 1 kg
salt, 18 g, (3 tsp)
garlic, 6 cloves
sugar, 30 g
ginger, 1
red pepper powder, 50 g (1.5 oz)
miso, 113 g (4 oz)
honey, 85 g (3 oz)
long red peppers, 2
Japanese plum, 4
Korean pear, Chinese pear or green apple
cranberries, 1 cup

Photo 4.23 Cutting radish.

1. Wash radishes, clean the skin gently with a sponge, don't use a brush. Cut half of the radishes into 2" long sections. Make vertical criss-cross cuts at 3/4" intervals. Stop cutting at about 1/2" (1 cm) from the bottom. Cut the remaining radishes into thin 2" long Julienne strips.

2. Soften radish by placing it for 3 hours in brine, that is made by dissolving 3 cups of salt (864 g) in 4 quarts (~ 4 liters) of water. Drain, rinse in fresh water, then drain again.

3. Mix miso, honey, red pepper powder, garlic and ginger. Use garlic press to squash ginger and garlic.

4. Spread the cut, insert a toothpick to keep it open and fill crevices with paste. Remove the toothpick and repeat the procedure at the next cut.

5. Cut the Korean pear into thin strips. Mix with dry cranberries and radish strips.

6. Place all strips on the bottom of a container and sprinkle salt over them. Mix. Place round sections of radishes on top.

7. Cover with cabbage leaves or inverted glass plate and apply some weight. You may fill a Ziplock® bag with brine and put it on top.

8. Ferment 3 days.

Photo 4.24 Stuffing radish.

Salted Vietnamese Cabbage

white cabbage, 1 kg
salt, 3%, 30 g
rice wine, 30 ml (2 Tbsp)
dried strips of seaweed, 28 g (1 oz)
fresh shrimp, 200 g (8 oz)

Photo 4.25 Dried seaweed.

1. Remove 2-3 outer cabbage leaves for later use.
Cut the cabbage into 6-8 wedges. Don't remove the core, just trim off the tough part. The core holds the leaves together.
2. Sprinkle a little salt into the bottom of the container or a bowl.
3. Place cabbage wedges, cut sides up. Sprinkle more salt on cabbage.
4. Pour over 1/2 cup (120 ml) of water.
5. Place a lid or inverted dinner plate on top of cabbage, then add a weight on top.
6. Let ferment for 3 days.
7. Drain and squeeze out the salty water.
8. Soak dry seaweed for 30 minutes in warm water. Drain and squeeze out water.
9. Boil shrimp for 2 minutes. Cool in tap water, drain, then cut into smaller pieces.
10. Mix seaweed with cabbage, shrimp, then pour rice wine over.
11. Place a light weight and let ferment for 3 days.
12. Store in refrigerator.

Salted White Cabbage

white cabbage, 1 kg
salt, 3%, 30 g
mirin (sweet rice wine), 30 ml (2 Tbsp)
seaweed sheets, 28 g (1 oz)

Photo 4.26 Dried kombu sheets can be cut into smaller squares.

1. Remove 2-3 outer cabbage leaves for later use.
Cut the cabbage into 6-8 wedges. Don't remove the core, just trim off the tough part. The core holds the leaves together.
2. Sprinkle a little salt into the bottom of the container or a bowl.
3. Place cabbage wedges, cut sides up. Sprinkle more salt on cabbage.
4. Pour over 1/2 cup (120 ml) of water.
5. Place a lid or inverted dinner plate on top of cabbage, then add weight on top.
6. Let ferment for 3 days.
7. Drain and squeeze out the salty water.
8. Mix with seaweed sheets and rice wine.
9. Place weight on top and let ferment for 3 days.
10. Store in refrigerator.

Pickled Cucumbers

There are two groups of pickled cucumbers:

- Fermented Pickles.
- Unfermented Pickles, also known as Quick Pickles or Fresh-Pack pickles.

Fermented Pickles

Genuine Fermented Dill Pickles are the best known type of pickles which are made by home and commercial producers. They are made with fresh cucumbers, salt, and spices. They are fermented in low salt brines, usually 5% or lower. Pickles fermented in low salt brines taste best but spoil sometimes and may have to be discarded. To avoid this risk commercial producers like to add some vinegar into the brine.

Fermented pickles owe their complex taste and flavor to the action of bacteria. The speed of the process is greatly influenced by the fermentation temperature and strength of the brine. The basic process has not changed much and the best genuine dill pickles are made using the same methods that were employed in the past. Poorly developed cucumbers may cause hollow pickles. Fermented pickles will usually be softer than fresh-pack pickles, but if fermented ones become too soft you probably did not remove all cucumber blossoms before you started to brine the cucumbers. Or, you may not have removed all the slime from the top of the brine as the cucumber fermented.

Fermentation

Cucumbers follow a lactic acid fermentation pattern similar to sauerkraut. Cucumbers are placed in the brine ensuring that none float on the surface. In the presence of air, the exposed cucumbers will react with yeasts and molds and white scum may develop. The salt in brine draws sugar and water out of cucumbers. As the cucumber contains around 90% water, a significant amount of cucumber water will mix with the brine making it weaker. Commercial producers readjust brine strength by adding more salt when needed. During fermentation cucumbers absorb salt. Due to this gradual absorption of salt, cucumbers become heavier and *they start to sink*. In two days they soften and the brine solution starts fermenting. Salt inhibits the growth of undesirable bacteria but lactic acid bacteria multiply and start consuming sugar which cucumbers contain inside. They break sugar into lactic acid, acetic acid and carbon dioxide gas (soda gas). If you are using a clear jar, you will see bubbles rising inside. The color changes from bright green to olive or yellow-green as acids react with the chlorophyll (a green pigment found in almost all plants). The tissue changes from solid white to translucent as air is forced out of the cells.

At the beginning of fermentation brine becomes cloudy due to bacteria growth and gas production. Brine may become clearer or remain cloudy which does not affect pickle quality in any way. It may not look visually pleasing but keep in mind that this cloudy brine contains all those complex flavors that are the product of fermentation. For better looks this brine could be filtered or replaced with a fresh clean brine of similar strength, but the wonderful flavor of the original brine will be gone.

cues

pakchoi

garlic

ginger

spr onion

basil

chillis

chilli pdr.

spice

mustard seed

whole allspice

coriander seed

cloves

gr ginger

chilli flakes

bay leaf

cinnamon stick

dill

turmeric

celery seeds

peppercorns

Photo 5.1 Cucumbers in fresh brine.

Photo 5.2 Two days later.

Photo 5.3 Four days later.

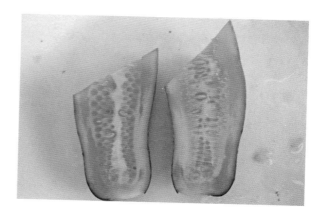

Photo 5.4 Semi-fermented pickle. As the fermentation progresses the texture of cucumber changes from opaque white to translucent. White areas signify incomplete fermentation. The photo depicts pickles which have been in brine for four days.

A cloudy brine or a white sediment may indicate the use of table salt rather than pickling salt. Table salt contains an anti-caking ingredient. Or it could also be that yeast has developed and settled to the bottom of the jar.

In most cases it is the result of a normal reaction during fermentation caused by the bacteria which produce fermentation. A small amount of white sediment is normal in a jar of firm pickles. However, if the pickles are soft, slippery or slimy, they may be spoiled so don't use them. You can eat partly fermented pickles after 3-4 days. They will still be deep green color, but the color will start turning olive green. After about three weeks, the cucumber flesh will become a translucent olive green. At this point, you can store them in a refrigerator or can them in jars. Cover with boiling hot brine that they were fermented in, and process pint jars for 10 minutes and quart jars for 15 minutes in a boiling water bath canner, if you live at altitudes below 1,000 feet.

Fermentation Temperature

Cucumbers ferment similarly to sauerkraut and for best results *Leuconostoc mesenteroides* bacteria should initiate fermentation. This calls for 64-72° F (18-22° C) temperature. Then *Lactobacillus plantarum* will take over the fermentation process. At those temperatures fermentation is accomplished in about 10 days. Then the container may be moved to a cooler place. If you like the taste of partly fermented pickles give them a try them after a few days of fermentation. Their taste will be somewhere in the middle between a fresh cucumber and fermented one. Pickles will continue to ferment but if you are satisfied with the taste, stop the fermentation by placing the container in a refrigerator.

Brine for Pickles

Too little salt lets undesirable bacteria grow rapidly. Too much salt slows down the fermentation process. The strength of the brine largely determines the taste of a pickle. Pickles made with lower salt brines result in better quality and contain less salt, a fact which is of much importance for people on a low salt diet. Cucumbers placed in low salt brines may exhibit a softer texture due to the enzymes which came from the cucumber itself, or yeasts and molds. Cucumbers placed in higher salt brines around 10% will develop a harder texture, but will be much saltier. Very salty brines (over 10%, 40 SAL) can prevent fermentation. As a general rule, fermentation takes place well in a brine of about 20° SAL (3/4 cup salt per gallon of water) and most people use this combination.

Typical brines:

% salt	°Sal	Salt per gallon of water	Salt Weight	Remarks
3.5	14	1/2 cup	144 g	half sour, fermentation accomplished in one week, not suitable for canning, keep refrigerated.
4	18	2/3 cup	192 g	half sour, not suitable for canning, keep refrigerated.
5	21	3/4 cup	216 g	sour, pickles fermented in 5% brine usually contain around 3% salt in a finished product, can be canned.
7-8	26-30	1 cup	288 g	very salty, long fermentation (6-8 weeks), *Lactobacillus plantarum* is the dominant bacteria strain, can be canned.

Seawater contains approximately 3.6% of salt which corresponds to 14 degrees salometer. Higher salt concentrations than >10% (>40° SAL) are not recommended as:

- Such high salt percentage inhibits lactic acid bacteria which may not ferment at all. This will result in very salty pickles which will have to be soaked in clean water before use.
- More bloaters (hollow-center pickles) may be produced.
- At 15% salt , 60° SAL, lactic bacteria cannot function, and no fermentation will take place.

Homemade Pickles

The best quality fermented pickles are made at home in a low salt brine without vinegar. This is how they were always made in Europe and by early settlers who came from Germany and Eastern European countries. Sometimes pickles spoiled and had to be discarded which was not something that commercial producers liked. To cut down on those losses and to extend the life of the product vinegar was added to brine. This made production easier and safer but it adversely affected the taste of the product.

What follows is the traditional method of making fermented pickles. Wash cucumbers of visible dirt but don't brush them off. There are some lactic acid bacteria present on the surface and they are needed to start fermentation. In the past, commercial producers did not wash cucumbers at all, but threw them into huge fermenting tanks. Remove all remnants of cucumber blossoms as molds and tissue softening enzymes are known to reside in those areas. You can cut about 1/16" (1.5 mm) off the ends of cucumbers, but scraping them off with a tip of a fingernail works fine.

Photo 5.5 Preparing all ingredients.

Photo 5.6 Cutting off cucumber blossom ends.

Place cucumbers in salt brine. Make sure all cucumbers are immersed in brine. Place sealed plastic Ziplock® bag filled with brine (4 ½ tablespoons salt and 3 quarts water) on top of cucumbers. If the bag spills its content this will not affect fermentation.

Photo 5.7 Ziplock® bag filled with water used as weight.

Photo 5.8 Ziplock® bag filled with brine.

Check pickles on a daily basis and remove any visible slime. Wash the bag and reinsert it in a fermenting crock. Let it ferment. An absence of gas bubbles signifies the end of fermentation.

Save some of the fermented cucumber juice as this is an excellent starter culture for the next production. Some claim, it is a great hangover cure. Strain the juice and pour it into dark bottles all the way to the top. This juice contains all minerals, vitamins and nutrients that lactic acid producing bacteria need to start a successful fermentation.

Yeasts and Molds

Yeasts and molds are of aerobic nature and will thrive in the presence of air, producing a white slime on the surface. This film should be skimmed off on a daily basis. To decrease the production of slime by yeasts, pickles should be covered with a sealed plastic bag filled with brine. This creates no-air conditions for yeasts and their growth is restricted.

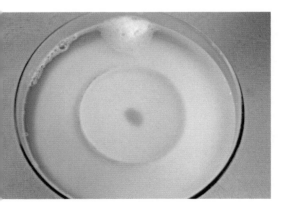

Photo 5.9 First traces of slime.

Photo 5.10 The slime should be discarded.

60

The bag can be removed and the slime wiped off. Then the clean bag is reinserted again. This takes care of the slime. What is harder to control are the tissue softening enzymes which were produced by the yeasts. Those enzymes will continue working and the pickle will be softer. Very salty brines decrease yeast production, adding vinegar is another effective measure. Pasteurization is the most effective preventive measure as it will kill most microorganisms.

Firming additives

- Alum – aluminum compound forms a firmer pickle. Alum is no longer recommended by the USDA as some people were having digestive problems.
- The calcium in lime improves pickle firmness.
- Turmeric is often added to improve color.
- Adding chopped horseradish root helps to keep pickled cucumbers crisp.
- When fermenting at low temperature adding oak leaves to brine helps to prevent spoilage. Oak leaves contain tannin acid which keeps spoilage bacteria at bay until fermenting bacteria produce enough lactic acid for the sauerkraut to be stable.

Home made pickles develop soft texture due to the enzymes that are present. The best fix to the problem is soaking cucumbers for 12-24 hours in a solution of 1 cup of food grade lime to 1 gallon of water. Excess lime absorbed by the cucumbers is removed by draining cucumbers, rinsing and then re-soaking them in fresh water for 1 hour. This rinsing and soaking step should be performed two more times.

Storing

Pickles made with low salt brines must be stored in a refrigerator in order to deactivate tissue softening enzymes, that may alter flavor, texture and color of the product. The product is usually consumed before any spoilage occurs. To prevent these problems in long storage, pickles should be processed in a boiling-water canner. Standard canning jars with self sealing lids are recommended.

Quick Pickles

Pickled cucumbers don't require much introduction, glass jars filled with different cucumber types stand on shelves in each supermarket. Billions of hamburgers are sold every year by fast food franchises and they contain a slice of a pickle inside. Canned pickles are subsequently pasteurized which eliminates oxygen by creating a vacuum inside the jar. This prevents molds and yeasts from growing. It also destroys tissue softening enzymes which create soft pickles. Quick pickles are made from fresh fruits and vegetables. *Quick pickles are not fermented.* Vinegar, sugar and spices are added. Then the pickles are pasteurized.

Quick pickling requires at least as much vinegar as other liquids. For pickling purpose brine, fruit or vegetable juice are all considered water and must be matched with an equal amount (or more) of vinegar. Acidity and the following pasteurizing step are the main safety precautions against pathogens so the amount of salt can now be decreased. According to USA standards, when the food is acidified to pH 4.6, the pathogenic bacteria spores cannot produce toxins.

It is important to use the proper vinegar to water ratio in preparing the brine. The brine should be at least one cup vinegar to each three parts of water. Failure to have a brine of this ratio can cause spoilage. Cucumbers no larger than six inches long will make the best pickles. Larger ones are likely to shrivel, or become hollow or soft. For the best results, pickle cucumbers within 24 hours. For the best results, pickle cucumbers within 24 hours after harvesting. At warm temperatures, cucumbers lose moisture rapidly, and don't produce a quality product. Certain small cucumbers, called *pickling cucumbers* are better for home pickling than the regular varieties. Shriveling is a problem which happens when the cucumber are placed in too strong a vinegar or vinegar-sugar solution. Cucumbers that are not freshly harvested are more likely to shrivel and become hollow, as are cucumbers you have harvested in very hot dry weather.

Canning Pickles

The following information pertains not only to pickled cucumbers, but to all other vegetables and fruits. The United States Department of Agriculture recommends processing pickles in boiling-water canners using the same techniques that are applied for making preserves. During the heat process oxygen will be eliminated and the resulting vacuum will prevent yeasts and molds from spoiling pickles.

Using boiling-water canners

Any general pot can be used as a canner as long as it is wide enough to accommodate removable perforated racks. It must be deep enough to cover the tops of jars with at least 1 inch of water during processing.

1. Fill the canner with enough water so it will be 1-2 inches over the top of filled jars.
2. Preheat water.
3. Load canner with filled jars, fitted with lids.
4. Add more boiling water, if needed, to cover jar tops.
5. Apply heat, cover the canner and maintain a boil throughout the process schedule.
6. Turn off the heat, remove the lid and wait 5 minutes before removing jars.
7. Leave the jars undisturbed to cool at room temperature for 12-24 hours.

Photo 5.11 Loading rack.

Photo 5.12 Boiling water canner.

Packing methods

Raw-packing is the method of filling jars tightly with freshly prepared, but *unheated* food. Such foods, especially fruit, will float in the jars. The entrapped air in and around the food may cause discoloration within 2-3 months of storage. Raw-packing is more suitable for vegetables processed in a pressure canner.

Hot-packing is the method of *heating* freshly prepared food to boiling, simmering it for 2-5 minutes, and promptly filling jars loosely with the boiled food. Whether food has been hot-packed or raw packed, the juice, syrup, or water to be added to the foods should also be heated to boiling before adding it to the jars. Hot-packing is the best way to remove air and is the preferred method for foods processed in a boiling-water canner.

Dill Pickles

Use the following quantities for each gallon capacity of your container.
4 lbs of 4-inch pickling cucumbers
2 tbsp dill seed or 4 to 5 heads fresh or dry dill weed
1/2 cup salt
1/4 cup vinegar (5%)
8 cups water and one or more of the following ingredients:
    2 cloves garlic (optional)
    2 dried red peppers (optional)
    2 tsp whole mixed pickling spices (optional)

Procedure: Wash cucumbers. Cut 1/16-inch slice off blossom end and discard. Leave 1/4-inch of stem attached. Place half of dill and spices on bottom of a clean, suitable container. Add cucumbers, remaining dill, and spices. Dissolve salt in vinegar and water and pour over cucumbers. Add suitable cover and weight. Store where temperature is between 70 and 75° F for about 3 to 4 weeks while fermenting. Temperatures of 55° to 65° F are acceptable, but the fermentation will take 5 to 6 weeks. Avoid temperatures above 80° F, or pickles will become too soft during fermentation. Fermenting pickles cure slowly. Check the container several times a week and promptly remove surface scum or mold. Caution: If the pickles become soft, slimy, or develop a disagreeable odor, discard them. Fully fermented pickles may be stored in the original container for about 4 to 6 months, provided they are refrigerated and surface scum and molds are removed regularly. *Canning fully fermented pickles is a better way to store them.* To can them, pour the brine into a pan, heat slowly to a boil, and simmer 5 minutes. Filter brine through paper coffee filters to reduce cloudiness, if desired. Fill hot jar with pickles and hot brine, leaving 1/2-inch headspace. Remove air bubbles and adjust headspace if needed. Wipe rims of jars with a dampened clean paper towel. Adjust lids and process as below:

Packing Method	Jar Size	Process Time in Minutes at Altitudes of		
		0-1000 ft	1,001-6,000 ft	Above 6,000 ft
Raw	Pints	10	15	20
	Quarts	15	20	25

Bread & Butter Pickles

6 lbs of 4 to 5-inch pickling cucumbers
8 cups thinly sliced onions (about 3 pounds)
1/2 cup canning or pickling salt
4 cups vinegar (5%)
4-1/2 cups sugar
2 tbsp mustard seed
1-1/2 tbsp celery seed
1 tbsp ground turmeric
1 cup pickling lime (optional) for use in variation below for making firmer pickles.

Yield: About 8 pints

Procedure: Wash cucumbers. Cut 1/16-inch off blossom end and discard. Cut into 3/16-inch slices. Combine cucumbers and onions in a large bowl. Add salt. Cover with 2 inches crushed or cubed ice. Refrigerate 3 to 4 hours, adding more ice as needed.

Combine remaining ingredients in a large pot. Boil 10 minutes. Drain and add cucumbers and onions and slowly reheat to boiling. Fill hot pint jars with slices and cooking syrup, leaving 1/2-inch headspace. Remove air bubbles and adjust headspace if needed. Wipe rims of jars with a dampened clean paper towel. Adjust lids and process as below:

Packing Method	Jar Size	Process Time in Minutes at Altitudes of		
		0-1000 ft	1,001-6,000 ft	Above 6,000 ft
Hot	Pints or Quarts	10	15	20

Photo 5.13 Bread & butter pickles, round slice.

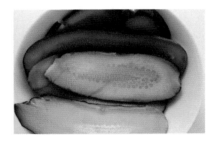

Photo 5.14 Bread & butter pickles, long slice.

64

Variation for firmer pickles: Wash cucumbers. Cut 1/16-inch off blossom end and discard. Cut into 3/16-inch slices. Mix 1 cup pickling lime and 1/2 cup salt to 1 gallon water in a 2 to 3 gallon crock or enamelware container. Caution: Avoid inhaling lime dust while mixing the lime water solution. Soak cucumber slices in lime water for 12 to 24 hours, stirring occasionally. Remove from lime solution, rinse, and resoak 1 hour in fresh cold water. Repeat the rinsing and soaking steps two more times. Handle carefully, as slices will be brittle. Drain well.

Storage: After processing and cooling, jars should be stored 4 to 5 weeks to develop ideal flavor.

Variation: Squash bread and butter pickles. Substitute slender (1 to 1-1/2 inches in diameter) zucchini or yellow summer squash for cucumbers.

Quick Fresh-Pack Dill Pickles

8 lbs of 3 to 5-inch pickling cucumbers
2 gals water
1-1/4 cups canning or picling salt (divided)
1-1/2 qts vinegar (5%)
1/4 cup sugar
2 qts water
2 tbsp whole mixed pickling spice
about 3 tbsp whole mustard seed (1 tsp per pint jar)
about 14 heads of fresh dill (1-1/2 heads per pint jar) or
4-1/2 tbsp dill seed (1-1/2 tsp per pint jar)

Yield: About 7 to 9 pints

Procedure: Wash cucumbers. Cut 1/16-inch slice off blossom end and discard, but leave 1/4 inch of stem attached. Dissolve 3/4 cup salt in 2 gallons water. Pour over cucumbers and let stand 12 hours. Drain. Combine vinegar, 1/2 cup salt, sugar, and 2 quarts water. Add mixed pickling spices tied in a clean white cloth. Heat to boiling. Fill hot jars with cucumbers. Add 1 tsp mustard seed and 1-1/2 heads fresh dill per pint. Cover with boiling pickling solution, leaving 1/2-inch headspace. Remove air bubbles and adjust headspace if needed. Wipe rims of jars with a dampened clean paper towel. Adjust lids and process as below:

Packing Method	Jar Size	Process Time in Minutes at Altitudes of		
		0-1000 ft	1,001-6,000 ft	Above 6,000 ft
Raw	Pints	10	15	20
	Quarts	15	20	25

Sweet Gherkin Pickles

7 lbs cucumbers (1-1/2 inch or less)
1/2 cup canning or pickling salt
8 cups sugar
6 cups vinegar (5%)
3/4 tsp turmeric
2 tsp celery seeds
2 tsp whole mixed pickling spice
2 cinnamon sticks
1/2 tsp fennel (optional)
2 tsp vanilla (optional)

Photo 5.15 Gherkin pickles.

Yield: About 6 to 7 pints

Procedure: Wash cucumbers. Cut 1/16-inch slice off blossom end and discard, but leave 1/4-inch of stem attached. Place cucumbers in large container and cover with boiling water. Six to 8 hours later, and again on the second day, drain and cover with 6 quarts of fresh boiling water containing 1/4 cup salt. On the third day, drain and prick cucumbers with a table fork. Combine and bring to a boil 3 cups vinegar, 3 cups sugar, turmeric, and spices. Pour over cucumbers. Six to 8 hours later, drain and save the pickling syrup. Add another 2 cups each of sugar and vinegar and reheat to boil. Pour over pickles. On the fourth day, drain and save syrup. Add another 2 cups sugar and 1 cup vinegar. Heat to boiling and pour over pickles. Drain and save pickling syrup 6 to 8 hours later. Add 1 cup sugar and 2 tsp vanilla and heat to boiling. Fill hot sterile pint jars with pickles and cover with hot syrup, leaving 1/2-inch headspace. Remove air bubbles and adjust headspace if needed. Wipe rims of jars with a dampened clean paper towel. Adjust lids and process as below:

Packing Method	Jar Size	Process Time in Minutes at Altitudes of		
		0-1000 ft	1,001-6,000 ft	Above 6,000 ft
Raw	Pints	5	10	15

14 Day Sweet Pickles

Can be canned whole, in strips, or in slices
4 lbs of 2 to 5-inch pickling cucumbers (if packed whole, use cucumbers of uniform size)
3/4 cup canning or pickling salt
(Separated - 1/4 cup of each of the 1st, 3rd, and 5th days)
2 tsp celery seed
2 tbsp mixed pickling spices
5-1/2 cups sugar
4 cups vinegar (5%)

Yield: About 5 to 9 pints

Procedure: Wash cucumbers. Cut 1/16-inch slice off blossom end and discard, but leave 1/4-inch of stem attached. Place whole cucumbers in suitable 1 gallon container. Add 1/4 cup canning or pickling salt to 2 quarts of water and bring to a boil. Pour over cucumbers. Add suitable cover and weight. Place clean towel over container and keep the temperature at about 70 F. On the third and fifth days, drain salt water and discard. Rinse cucumbers and rescald cover and weight. Return cucumbers to container. Add 1/4 cup salt to 2 quarts fresh water and boil. Pour over cucumbers. Replace cover and weight, and re-cover with clean towel. On the seventh day, drain salt water and discard. Rinse cucumbers and rescald containers, cover, and weight. Slice or strip cucumbers if desired, and return to container. Place celery seed and pickling spices in small cheesecloth bag. Combine 2 cups sugar and 4 cups vinegar in a saucepan. Add spice bag, bring to a boil and pour pickling solution over cucumbers. Add cover and weight, and re-cover with clean towel. On each of the next six days, drain syrup and spice bag and save. Add 1/2 cup sugar each day and bring to a boil in a saucepan. Remove cucumbers and rinse. Scald container, cover, and weight daily. Return cucumbers to container, add boiled syrup, cover, weight, and re-cover with towel. On the 14th day, drain syrup into saucepan. Fill hot sterile pint jars or clean hot quart jars, leaving 1/2-inch headspace. Add 1/2 cup sugar to syrup and bring to boil. Remove spice bag. Pour hot syrup over cucumbers, leaving 1/2-inch headspace. Remove air bubbles and adjust headspace if needed. Wipe rims of jars with a dampened clean paper towel. Adjust lids and process as below:

Packing Method	Jar Size	Process Time in Minutes at Altitudes of		
		0-1000 ft	1,001-6,000 ft	Above 6,000 ft
Raw	Pints	5	10	15
	Quarts	10	15	20

Quick Sweet Pickles

May be canned as either strips or slices

8 lbs of 3 to 4-inch picling cucumbers
1/3 cup canning or pickling salt
4-1/2 cups sugar
3-1/2 cups vinegar (5%)
2 tsp celery seed
1 tbsp whole allspice
2 tbsp mustard seed
1 cup pickling lime (optional) for use in variation below for making firmer pickles
Yield: About 7 to 9 pints

Procedure: Wash cucumbers. Cut 1/16-inch off blossom end and discard, but leave 1/4 inch of stem attached. Slice or cut in strips, if desired. Place in bowl and sprinkle with 1/3 cup salt. Cover with 2 inches of crushed or cubed ice. Refrigerate 3 to 4 hours. Add more ice as needed. Drain well. Combine sugar, vinegar, celery seed, allspice, and mustard seed in 6-quart kettle. Heat to boiling.

Hot pack - Add cucumbers and heat slowly until vinegar solution returns to boil. Stir occasionally to make sure mixture heats evenly. Fill sterile jars, leaving 1/2-inch headspace.

Raw pack - Fill hot jars, leaving 1/2-inch headspace. Add hot pickling syrup, leaving 1/2-inch headspace.

Remove air bubbles and adjust headspace if needed. Wipe rims of jars with a dampened clean paper towel. Adjust lids and process as below:

Packing Method	Jar Size	Process Time in Minutes at Altitudes of		
		0-1000 ft	1,001-6,000 ft	Above 6,000 ft
Raw	Pints	10	15	20
	Quarts	15	20	25
Hot	Pints or Quarts	5	10	15

Variation for firmer pickles: Wash cucumbers. Cut 1/16-inch off blossom end and discard, but leave 1/4-inch of stem attached. Slice or strip cucumbers. Mix 1 cup pickling lime and 1/2 cup salt to 1 gallon water in a 2 to 3 gallon crock or enamelware container. Caution: Avoid inhaling lime dust while mixing the lime water solution. Soak cucumber slices or strips in lime water solution for 12 to 24 hours, stirring occasionally. Remove from lime solution and rinse and resoak 1 hour in fresh cold water. Repeat the rinsing and resoaking two more times. Handle carefully because slices or strips will be brittle. Drain well.

Notes:

Commonly added spices: dill, mustard seeds, celery seed, allspice, turmeric.

When held in a cool dark place at 72° F (22° C) or lower, sealed jars can be stored for one year without losing quality.

Use a commercially manufactured 5 percent acidity (50 grain) white vinegar. Other vinegars have a good flavor and aroma, but may darken white or light colored fruits and vegetables.

Pickles And Relishes

In addition to cabbage and cucumbers, other vegetables can be successfully naturally fermented. Root vegetables such as radish, turnip, and beets are very healthy and ferment easily with salt alone. They will retain all nutrients, minerals and vitamins as long as they are not subjected to thermal processing.

Pickled Vegetables And Fruits

Pickles are made from fruits and vegetables or their combinations. They are preserved with vinegar, lemon juice or citric acid. Bacteria will not grow in strong acidic environment and this rule applies to fruits, vegetables and fast fermented meat products. The natural fermentation is a lengthy process and to preserve foods fast we have to increase acidity of the product by other methods. Generally, pickled foods are made with vinegar in varying proportions and are canned in glass jars using the boiling water processing. Vinegar imparts a characteristic acidic flavor which is usually offset by the careful selection of fruits and adding sugar. Pickled foods are classified into the following groups:

- Fermented Pickles - usually cucumbers, but other vegetables may be employed. Vegetables are placed in a salt solution for several weeks until fermented. Curing time largely depends on temperature. During this time, changes in color, flavor and texture take place.

- Unfermented Pickles, also known as Quick Pickles or Fresh Pack Pickles. The vinegar in the recipe preserves the fruit or vegetable. You can make vegetables directly into pickles without soaking in salt brine, or you can soak them a short time.

- Relishes - fruits, vegetables or their combinations. Sweet relishes contain more sugar. Pickles and relishes are very similar. For pickles, you leave vegetables whole, or cut them according to the recipe. For relishes, however, you chop vegetables and/or fruits before you put them into a vinegar mixture.

- Fruit Pickles - whole or sliced fruits like peaches, pears, watermelons, figs and other fruits are heated in a spicy sweet-sour syrup.

- Chutneys - fruit and vegetables or their combinations. Chutneys are usually strongly spiced.

- Sauce - usually vegetables, they can be mild or hot. Very popular sauces can be pickled such as Tomato Ketchup Sauce, Chili Sauce, Red Pepper Sauce, Taco Sauce and others.

- Sweet pickles are prepared in much the same manner as other pickles, except that vinegar is sweetened and more spices are added. Sometimes portions of vinegar are drained and sweet spicy liquid is added a little at a time until the desired sweetness is obtained.

Quick pickles are made from fresh fruits and vegetables. *Quick pickles are not fermented.* Vinegar, sugar and spices are added. Then the pickles are pasteurized. Quick pickling requires at least as much vinegar as other liquids. For pickling purpose brine, fruit or vegetable juice are all considered water and must be matched with an equal amount (or more) of vinegar. The United States Department of Agriculture (USDA) recommends that homemade pickles contain at least 70% acetic acid (pH 4.0 or less).

Fermented Pickles

Photo 6.1 Beets.

Beets

Beets rich chemical and mineral composition has made them a medicinal vegetable for thousands of years. Beets are rich in nitrates and when consumed regularly, they help to lower blood pressure and stimulate the immune system. Beet juice is a powerful natural colorant.

beets, 1 kg (2.2 lb)
salt, 2.5%, 25 g (4 tsp
whole cloves, 4
cinnamon stick, 1, crushed
sugar, 15 g (1 Tbsp)
400 g, Korean or Chinese Ya pear, or an apple.

1. Cut off stalks and rinse beets off to get rid of dirt. Don't scrub the outside or peel the beets.
2. Slice or grate beets. Cut pears into wedges.
3. Mix with salt and spices.
4. Pack. Place a weight on top. Beets may get foamy, this is normal.
5. Ferment, preferably around 68° F (20° C), for about 2 weeks. After 3 days, taste the beets and see how you like them. If you want them a little tangier, let them ferment longer. If you like what you taste, refrigerate.

Photo 6.2 Fermented beets.

Fermented Beets and Horseradish Relish

Finely grated fresh beets and horseradish is a great combination that goes well with cold meat cuts. Horseradish is a root crop, grown for the pungent roots. They contain highly volatile oils with a sharp flavor. Grind fresh horseradish in a well-ventilated room. The fumes from grinding are potent. If you use a manual grater expect to cry a lot! Beets will color your hands purple, so use gloves.

Photo 6.3 Horseradish.

beets, 700 g (1.54 lb)
salt, 2.5%, 25 g (4 tsp)
horseradish, 200 g (0.5 lb)
caraway seeds, 1 tsp
sugar, 15 g (1 Tbsp)

1. Wash and rinse beets to get rid of dirt but don't scrub the outside or peel them. Slice or grate.
2. Do the same with horseradish.
3. Mix everything with spices, salt and sugar.
4. Pack in a container. Place weight on top.
5. Ferment, preferably around 68° F (20° C), for about 2 weeks. Serve with lemon wedges.

Photo 6.4 Beet relish.

Turnips

Fermented turnip known also as "Sauerruben" is made exactly as sauerkraut.

white turnips, 1 kg (2.2 lb)
salt, 2.5%, 25 g (4 tsp)

1. Rinse turnips off to get rid of dirt but don't scrub the outside or peel the skin. There are microorganisms living on the outside of the beets that will start the fermentation process.
2. Slice or grate turnips.
3. Mix with salt.
4. Pack. Place a weight on top.
5. Ferment, preferably around 68° F (20° C), for about 2 weeks.

Note: you may add a teaspoon of caraway or mustard seeds for flavor.

White Daikon Radish

daikon, 1 kg (2.2 lb)
salt, 2.5%, 25 g (4 tsp)
scalions, 5 stalks
garlic, 5 cloves
fresh ginger, 1 slice,
peeled and diced.
ground hot pepper, 1 tsp

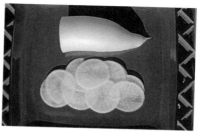

Photo 6.5 Daikon radish.

1. Rinse daikon off to get rid of dirt but don't scrub the outside or peel the skin. There are microorganisms living on the outside of the beets that will start the fermentation process.
2. Slice radishes into thin strips or dice finely. Cut scallions into rounds. Mince garlic.
3. Mix all ingredients with salt.
4. Pack. Place a weight on top.
5. Ferment, preferably around 68° F (20° C), for 7 days.

Note:
After 3 days radishes taste great and may be packed and refrigerated.

Quick Pickles

Pickled Beets
7 lbs of 2 to 2-1/2 inch diameter beets
4 cups vinegar (5%)
1-1/2 tsp canning or pickling salt
2 cups sugar
2 cups water
2 cinnamon sticks
12 whole cloves
4 to 6 onions (2 to 2-1/2 inch diameter), if desired

Yield: About 8 pints.

Procedure: Trim off beet tops, leaving 1 inch of stem and roots to prevent bleeding of color. Wash thoroughly. Sort for size. Cover similar sizes together with boiling water and cook until tender (about 25 to 30 minutes). Caution: Drain and discard liquid. Cool beets.

Trim off roots and stems and slip off skins. Slice into 1/4 inch slices. Peel and thinly slice onions. Combine vinegar, salt, sugar, and fresh water. Put spices in cheesecloth bag and add to vinegar mixture. Bring to a boil. Add beets and onions. Simmer 5 minutes. Remove spice bag. Fill hot jars with beets and onions, leaving 1/2 inch headspace. Add hot vinegar solution, allowing 1/2 inch headspace. Remove air bubbles and adjust headspace if needed. Wipe rims of jars with a dampened clean paper towel. Adjust lids and process.

Packing Method	Jar Size	Process Time in Minutes at Altitudes of			
		0-1000 ft	1,001-3,000 ft	3,001-6,000 ft	Above 6,000 ft
Hot	Pints or quarts	30	35	40	45

Variation: For pickled whole baby beets, follow above directions but use beets that are 1 to 1-1/2 inches in diameter. Pack whole; do not slice. Onions may be omitted.

Pickled Carrots

2-3/4 lbs peeled carrots (about 3-1/2 lbs as purchased)
5-1/2 cups white vinegar (5%)
1 cup water
2 cups sugar
2 tsp canning salt
8 tsp mustard seed
4 tsp celery seed

Yield: About 4 pints.

Procedure: Wash and peel carrots. Cut into rounds that are approximately 1/2 inch thick. Combine vinegar, water, sugar and canning salt in an 8 quart Dutch oven or stockpot. Bring to a boil and boil 3 minutes. Add carrots and bring back to a boil. Then reduce heat to a simmer and heat until half cooked (about 10 minutes). Meanwhile, place 2 teaspoons mustard seed and 1 teaspoon celery seed into each empty hot pint jar. Fill jars with hot carrots, leaving 1 inch headspace. Fill with hot pickling liquid, leaving 1/2 inch headspace. Remove air bubbles and adjust headspace if needed. Wipe rims of jars with a dampened clean paper towel. Adjust lids and process.

Packing Method	Jar Size	Process Time in Minutes at Altitudes of		
		0-1000 ft	1,001-6,000 ft	Above 6,000 ft
Hot	Pints	15	20	25

Relishes

A relish is a cooked, pickled, or chopped vegetable or fruit food item typically used as a condiment in particular to enhance a staple. Examples are jams, chutneys, and the North American "relish," a pickle cucumber jam eaten with hot dogs or hamburgers. In the United States, the most common commercially available relishes are made from pickled cucumbers and are known in the food trade as pickle relishes. Two variants of this are hamburger relish (pickle relish in a ketchup base or sauce) and hotdog relish (pickle relish in a mustard base or sauce). A very popular Polish combination of beets and horseradish ("Cwikla") ia a type of relish.

Pickle Relish

3 qts chopped cucumbers
3 cups each of chopped sweet green and red peppers
1 cup chopped onions
3/4 cup canning or pickling salt
4 cups ice
8 cups water
2 cups sugar
4 tsp each of mustard seed, turmeric, whole allspice,
and whole cloves
6 cups white vinegar (5%)

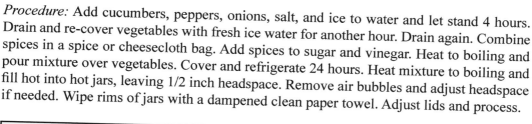

Photo 6.6 Cucumber relish.

Yield: About 9 pints.

Procedure: Add cucumbers, peppers, onions, salt, and ice to water and let stand 4 hours. Drain and re-cover vegetables with fresh ice water for another hour. Drain again. Combine spices in a spice or cheesecloth bag. Add spices to sugar and vinegar. Heat to boiling and pour mixture over vegetables. Cover and refrigerate 24 hours. Heat mixture to boiling and fill hot into hot jars, leaving 1/2 inch headspace. Remove air bubbles and adjust headspace if needed. Wipe rims of jars with a dampened clean paper towel. Adjust lids and process.

Packing Method	Jar Size	Process Time in Minutes at Altitudes of		
		0-1000 ft	1,001-6,000 ft	Above 6,000 ft
Hot	½ Pints or Pints	5	10	15

Picalilli

From Wikepedia:

Piccalilli is a British relish of chopped pickled vegetables and spices. British piccalilli contains various vegetables— invariably cauliflower and vegetable marrow —and seasonings of mustard and turmeric. It is used as an accompaniment to foods such as sausages, bacon, eggs, toast, cheese, and tomatoes.

In the Northeastern United States, commercial piccalillis are based on diced sweet peppers, either red or green. This style is very similar to sweet pepper relish, with the piccalilli being distinguished by having a darker red or green color and like British piccalilli, the chunks are larger and it is tangier and less sweet. It is a popular topping on such foods as hamburgers and hot dogs.

In the Midwestern United States, commercial piccalillis are based on finely chopped gherkins; bright green and on the sweet side, they are often used as a condiment for Chicago-style hot dogs. This style is sometimes called "neon relish".

In the Southern United States, piccalilli is less popular. In its place, chow-chow, a relish with a base of chopped green (unripe) tomatoes is offered. This relish may also include onions, bell peppers, cabbage, green beans and other vegetables. While not exactly similar to other piccalillis, chow-chow is often called as such and the terms may be used interchangeably.

6 cups chopped green tomatoes
1-1/2 cups chopped sweet red peppers
1-1/2 cups chopped green peppers
2-1/4 cups chopped onions
7-1/2 cups chopped cabbage
1/2 cup canning or pickling salt
3 Tbsp whole mixed pickling spice
4-1/2 cups vinegar (5%)
3 cups brown sugar

Photo 6.7 Picalilli.

Yield: About 9 half pints.

Procedure: Wash, chop, and combine vegetables with 1/2 cup salt. Cover with hot water and let stand 12 hours. Drain and press in a clean white cloth to remove all possible liquid. Tie spices loosely in a spice bag and add to combined vinegar and brown sugar and heat to a boil in a sauce pan. Add vegetables and boil gently 30 minutes or until the volume of the mixture is reduced by one half. Remove spice bag. Fill hot sterile jars with hot mixture, leaving 1/2 inch headspace. Remove air bubbles and adjust headspace if needed. Wipe rims of jars with a dampened clean paper towel. Adjust lids and process.

Packing Method	Jar Size	Process Time in Minutes at Altitudes of		
		0-1000 ft	1,001-6,000 ft	Above 6,000 ft
Hot	½ Pints or Pints	5	10	15

Chutneys

From Wikipedia:

Chutney is a condiment used in South Asian cuisine that usually contains a spice and vegetable mix. There is no limit to the number of chutneys as it can be made from virtually any vegetable/fruit/herb/spices or a combination of them. Chutneys come in two major groups, sweet and hot; both forms usually contain various spices, including chili, but differ by their main flavour. Chutney types and their preparations vary widely across Pakistan and India. American and European styled chutneys are usually fruit, vinegar and sugar, cooked down to a reduction. Flavorings are always added to the mix. These may include sugar, salt, garlic, tamarind, onion, or ginger.
Spices most commonly include fenugreek, coriander, cumin and asafoetida (hing).

Mango Chutney

11 cups or 4 lbs chopped unripe (hard) mango
2-1/2 cups or 3/4 lb finely chopped yellow onion
2-1/2 Tbsp grated fresh ginger
1-1/2 Tbsp finely chopped fresh garlic
4-1/2 cups sugar
3 cups white distilled vinegar (5%)
2-1/2 cups golden raisins
1 tsp canning salt
4 tsp chili powder

Photo 6.8 Mango chutney.

Caution: Handling green mangoes may irritate the skin of some people in the same way as poison ivy. (They belong to the same plant family.) To avoid this reaction, wear plastic or rubber gloves while working with raw green mango. Do not touch your face, lips or eyes after touching or cutting raw green mangoes until all traces are washed away.

Yield: About 6 half pint jars.

Procedure: Wash, peel, and separate mango flesh from seed. Chop mango flesh into chunks and puree in blender or food processor until smooth. Combine all ingredients in a 6 to 8 quart Dutch oven or stockpot and heat on medium high heat, with continuous stirring, until the mixture reaches 200 F. The mixture will sputter as it is being heated, so be sure to wear gloves or oven mitts to avoid burning skin. Fill hot sauce into hot half pint jars, leaving 1/4 inch headspace. Remove air bubbles and adjust headspace if needed. Wipe rims of jars with a dampened clean paper towel. Adjust lids and process.

Packing Method	Jar Size	Process Time in Minutes at Altitudes of		
		0-1000 ft	1,001-6,000 ft	Above 6,000 ft
Hot	½ Pints or Pints	10	15	20

Chow-Chow

Chow-chow is a Nova Scotian and American pickled relish made from a combination of vegetables. Mainly green tomato, cabbage, chayote, red tomatoes, onions, carrots, beans, asparagus, cauliflower and peas are used. These ingredients are pickled in a canning jar and served cold. Chow-chow found its way to the Southern United States during the expulsion of the Acadian people from Nova Scotia and their settlement in Louisiana.

Chow-Chow Relish

1 chopped cabbage
2 cups sliced cucumbers
2 quarts vinegar
1 gallon water
2 cups salt
sliced onions, 2 cups
chopped green tomatoes, 2 cup
chopped sweet peppers, 2 cups
3 cups sugar
1tsp. cayenne pepper
2 Tbsp celery seed
2 Tbsp mustard seed
1 Tbsp of turmeric

Photo 6.9 Chow-chow.

1. Place cabbage, cucumbers, tomatoes and onions in brine (1 gal of water & 2 cups salt) overnight. Drain.
2. Mix all vegetables with remaining ingredients and boil for 10 minutes.
3. Pack hot into hot pint jars, leaving 1/2 inch headspace. Remove air bubbles, wipe jar rims. Place lids and screw bands. Process 10 minutes in a Boiling Water Bath.

Packing Method	Jar Size	Process Time in Minutes at Altitudes of		
		0-1000 ft	1,001-6,000 ft	Above 6,000 ft
Hot	½ Pints or Pints	10	15	20

Pickled Horseradish Sauce

2 cups (3/4 lb) freshly grated
horseradish
1 cup white vinegar (5%)
1/2 tsp canning or pickling salt
1/4 tsp powdered ascorbic acid
(vitamin C)

Yield: About 2 half pints.

Photo 6.10 Horseradish sauce.

Procedure: The pungency of fresh horseradish fades within 1 to 2 months, even when refrigerated. Therefore, make only small quantities at a time. Wash horseradish roots thoroughly and peel off brown outer skin. The peeled roots may be grated in a food processor or cut into small cubes and put through a food grinder. *Combine ingredients and fill into glass jars*, leaving 1/4 inch headspace. Seal jars tightly and store in a refrigerator.

Pickled Beets & Horseradish Sauce

2 cups (3/4 lb) freshly
grated beets
2 cups (3/4 lb) freshly
grated horseradish
1 cup white vinegar (5%)
1 tsp canning or pickling salt
1/4 tsp powdered ascorbic acid
(vitamin C)

Yield: About 2 half pints.

Photo 6.11 Beet & horseradish sauce.

Procedure: The pungency of fresh horseradish fades within 1 to 2 months, even when refrigerated. Therefore, make only small quantities at a time. Wash horseradish roots thoroughly and peel off brown outer skin. The peeled roots may be grated in a food processor or cut into small cubes and put through a food grinder. *Combine ingredients and fill into glass jars*, leaving 1/4 inch headspace. Seal jars tightly and store in a refrigerator.

Note: grating horseradish induces a lot of tears, so do it in a well ventilated area, or use a food processor. Wash and peel the root as you would a potato and dice it into small cubes. Place the cubes in the blender. Completely cover the blades with cold water or crushed ice before you turn the blender on. When done, pour off excess water.

Photo 6.12 Grating horseradish.

Useful Links

Equipment & Supplies

The Sausage Maker Inc., equipment & supplies
www.sausagemaker.com

Mid-Western Research & Supply Inc., equipment & supplies
http://www.midwesternresearch.com

Allied Kenco Sales, equipment & supplies
www.alliedkenco.com

Grainger, rubber grommets
www.grainger.com

Eden Foods, kombu, kirin, supplies
www.edenfoods.com

American Weigh Scales Inc., digital scales
http://www.awscales.com

Container & Packaging Supply, glass jars
http://www.containerandpackaging.com

Canning Pantry, canning supplies
http://www.canningpantry.com

Information

USDA Guides to Home Canning
http://ndb.nal.usda.gov

US National Nutrient Database
http://ndb.nal.usda.gov/ndb/foods/list

Calorie Control Council
http://www.caloriecontrol.org

USDA Agricultural Research Service
http://www.ars.usda.gov/main/main.htm

Other Books by Stanley & Adam Marianski

Home Production of Quality Meats & Sausages bridges the gap that exists between highly technical textbooks and the requirements of the typical hobbyist. The book covers topics such as curing and making brines, smoking meats and sausages, making special sausages such as head cheeses, blood and liver sausages, hams, bacon, butts, loins, safety and more...

ISBN: 978-0-9824267-3-9

Meat Smoking & Smokehouse Design explains differences between grilling, barbecuing and smoking. There are extensive discussions of curing as well as the particulars about smoking sausages, meat, fish, poultry and wild game.

ISBN: 978-0-9824267-0-8

The Art Of Making Fermented Sausages shows readers how to control meat acidity and removal of moisture, choose proper temperatures for fermenting, smoking and drying, understand and control fermentation process, choose proper starter cultures and make traditional or fast-fermented products, choose proper equipment, and much more...

ISBN: 978-0-9824267-1-5

Polish Sausages contains government recipes that were used by Polish meat plants between 1950 - 1990. These recipes come from government manuals that were never published before, which are now revealed in great detail.

ISBN: 978-0-9824267-2-2

Making Healthy Sausages reinvents traditional sausage making by introducing a completely new way of thinking. The reader will learn how to make a product that is nutritional and healthy, yet delicious to eat. The collection of 80 recipes provides a valuable reference on the structure of reduced fat products.

ISBN: 978-0-9836973-0-5

The Amazing Mullet offers information that has been gathered through time and experience. Successful methods of catching, smoking and cooking fish are covered in great depth and numerous filleting, cleaning, cooking and smoking practices are reviewed thoroughly. In addition to mullet recipes, detailed information on making fish cakes, ceviche, spreads and sauces are also included.

ISBN: 978-0-9824267-8-4

2985022R00044

Made in the USA
San Bernardino, CA
23 June 2013